HONG KONG MONEY

How Chinese Families and Fortunes are Changing Canada

JOHN DeMONT
THOMAS FENNELL

Canadian Cataloguing in Publication Data

DeMont, John
    Hong Kong money

ISBN 1-55013-164-8

1. Hong Kong – Emigration and immigration – Economic aspects. 2. Hong Kong – Economic conditions. I. Fennell, Thomas II. Title.

HC470.3.F46 1989   330.951'25   C89-094099-1

Key Porter Books Limited
70 The Esplanade
Toronto, Ontario
M5E 1R2

Design: D. Maxwell
Typesetting: Computer Composition

Printed and bound in Canada by
T. H. Best Printing Company Limited

89 90 91 92 93 6 5 4 3 2 1

CONTENTS

Acknowledgments / v

Introduction / 1

1. Hong Kong: The Boiler Room of Capitalism / 7

2. Li Ka-shing: The New *Taipan* / 29

3. Ho and The Three Musketeers / 53

4. Chasing Hong Kong Money / 79

5. Toronto: A City for the Taking / 109

6. Vancouver: A City Divided / 139

7. Building a Capitalist Bridge / 171

Index / 209

ACKNOWLEDGMENTS

Hong Kong Money began in the spring of 1987 when *Maclean's* magazine sent Thomas Fennell to Hong Kong to profile billionaire industrialist Li Ka-shing. On his return, Fennell's desire to write the continuing and growing story surrounding the exodus of people and money out of Hong Kong was ignited by Key Porter Books' own enthusiasm for the book.

Fennell joined with *Maclean's* senior writer John DeMont to write the book, and Ann Walmsley — one of Canada's top business journalists — who reported a broad piece of it. Ann's aggressive and thorough reporting would prove invaluable. As the winter of 1988 progressed, the trio pushed deeper and deeper into their subject, with Fennell again departing for Hong Kong, DeMont to Ottawa and Walmsley to Toronto's and Vancouver's Chinatowns.

INTRODUCTION

High in the open ranges of the executive offices of the Hong Kong & Shanghai Banking Corporation in Hong Kong, a bank executive muses that, for the colony's elite and rich middle class, paying $250,000 for a Canadian passport is a deal: "they carry that much in their back pocket." Far below, on a crowded freeway that slices by the harbor in the Wan Chai district, a taxi driver also knows about the escape to Canada. He says, optimistically: "I hope to join my family in Canada."

Two views of Canada: one from a member of the powerful elite who can simply buy the way into Canada under one of an assortment of greedy provincial programs, and the other, just a whisper in a chorus of 1.1 billion Chinese voices that knows about the affluent country across the ocean, and is determined to get there. They represent two aspects of the reality that is propelling a tidal wave of cash and people from the old British colony to Canada. On the one hand, there are those who are frantically moving assets across the ocean and out of the reach of communist authorities; on the other hand, there are many

Hong Kong residents who simply long to start life over in a secure, less competitive society.

Hong Kong Money explores the politics behind this wave of Chinese immigration. In Beijing, Hong Kong, Ottawa and the provincial capitals, one of the great events of modern history, the return of Hong Kong to China in 1997, is being weighed and analysed for tactical advantage. At the root of the emotional debate over Hong Kong, on both sides of the Pacific Ocean, is money. What to do with the billions of dollars (it is estimated that as much as $10 billion in cash is set to flee Hong Kong at any given time) before the Chinese People's Liberation Army arrives?

For the people of Hong Kong, as the killing of the students in Beijing's Tiananmen Square so brutally illustrated, their fortunes, if not their lives, are at risk in the shifting, and as often as not, cruel tide of Chinese politics. On the other side of the Pacific, far away from Hong Kong's boiling, profit-driven environment, another view of the Chinese takeover is taken by detached lawyers (sometimes corrupt) who are waiting to cash in on the rising level of fear in the colony, by helping to move fortunes and people into Canada. Provincial politicians and bureaucrats, too, hope to tap that same flow of money and people to create new commerce in their provinces. To capture the best — lately that simply means "the richest" — of the immigrants, Canada's provinces have waged war against one another with programs that offer Canadian citizenship at fire-sale prices — a fact that greatly bothers some immigration officials in Hong Kong. Access to an economically poor province like New Brunswick can be bought for $150,000 while entry to relatively richer turf, like Quebec, costs $250,000.

While the cheap passport policy may appear unseemly and even disgust many Canadians (it is a source of great amusement in Hong Kong's corporate towers) we believe that this latest wave of immigration will pay great dividends to Canada as Hong Kong moves closer and closer to 1997. As the century draws to a close, Canada's, Hong Kong's and China's economies will be linked by a flesh-and-blood bridge of perhaps as many as 200,000 new Hong Kong refugees. Clearly, Canada's hardening links to Hong Kong will ensure that it is the great beneficiary of the opening up of the Chinese economy. In fact, no other country has thrown its gates open as wide to Hong Kong residents as has Canada.

By detailing the activities of four of Hong Kong's richest citizens — Stanley Ho, Li Ka-shing, Cheng Yu-tung and Lee Shau-kee — and dozens of lesser corporate barons, we show that the communist Chinese plan to use the colony's economic punch to dramatically speed up their own long-anticipated economic modernization. Canada, with its extensive and growing links to the Hong Kong Chinese, particularly this powerful foursome, will find itself on the front lines of this revolution in world commerce.

Hong Kong Money shows how the so-called Hong Kong billionaires' club — the colony's richest men — has run out of investment opportunities on its home field, while its income, particularly the influx of American dollars, continues unabated. Li Ka-shing and his two Canadian sons, for example, may control more than 30 per cent of everything that moves on the Hong Kong Stock Exchange. Some analysts claim that, at any given moment, Li has nearly $5 billion to invest somewhere in the world. Currently, both Canadian energy stocks and real estate are attracting the Asian tycoons. In many cases, particularly since the terrible events in Beijing, Hong Kong's richest citizens are following Li's example and sending their families here to administer their assets. This means not only that scores of new businesses are opening in Canada, but also that these aggressive Chinese Canadians are injecting a new spirit of entrepreneurship into Canadian business.

In fact, the effort to move assets to Canada, and out of the reach of the communist Chinese, has become so frantic that many high-flying residents of the colony are attempting to change their assets into blue-chip Canadian stocks. (Incredibly, some complain that the Toronto Stock Exchange cannot generate enough volume to satisfy them.) Others are filling bank vaults with hard assets, from bearer bonds to platinum watches. And, of course, there is always Canadian real estate.

This is not to say that a simple desire to live in a secure, free country does not also lie behind the exodus. Many young members of Hong Kong families are thriving as new Canadians. Thousands of young Chinese immigrants who came to Canada to attend school have stayed by choice. But even they eventually become conduits for cash and other hard assets, and for other Hong Kong immigrants under family reunification programs.

Hong Kong Money shows how these Chinese Canadians have found the Canadian economy full of opportunities that traditional Canadian business people have missed. Their story is not restricted to the booming cities of Vancouver and Toronto. It is growing daily in all regions of Canada — even the economically troubled areas. For example, look no farther than the HongKong Bank of Canada office in Halifax. The office is located in Historic Properties, an area of restored eighteenth-century buildings and warehouses on the waterfront. Perhaps symbolically, the area used to be the economic centre of the colony, and was home to many of the merchant banks that later became part of Canada's large chartered banking system. Now it consists just of tourist shops and a few offices, but the presence of the Hong Kong Bank is a sign of their growing interest in the Maritimes.

Until the events in Tiananmen Square in the spring of 1989, many experts on Hong Kong, and executives toiling for the colony's powerful elite, argued that money and people would be safe there after 1997. But the carnage in Beijing and continuing repression have dealt a major blow to their confidence in the future stability of Hong Kong — ensured that even more money flows to Canada. Indeed, as automatic weapons sprayed bullets across the Square, people lined up in Hong Kong to withdraw money from banks with links to China. Ironically, the run on these banks came as the communist giant was buying up more and more of the colony, and was about to open the Bank of China's new headquarters there. In a rare display of public unity, legislators and members of Hong Kong governor Sir David Wilson's advisory executive council issued a statement: "In Hong Kong, no matter how angry we are, we must put all our energies into preserving the separateness of our system. . . . Our future depends on the maintenance of our existing system and our continued stability."

There was little faith that the system could be preserved. Indeed at the start of the day's trading following the rioting in Beijing, on the Hong Kong Stock Exchange, when it was obvious that the market was about to crash, the Secretary for Monetary Affairs, David Nendick, said: "If you are in stocks and shares, stay there; you are certainly not going to get a reasonable value for your shares just now." But no one in cash-conscious Hong Kong listened, and the Heng Seng Index of blue-chip companies (most controlled by a few Hong Kong billionaires) fell 581.77 points, or more than 21 per cent. "I'm afraid what's happening in Beijing can only be seen as a major blow to Hong Kong's hopes for stability," said one diplomat. "With that kind of behavior, you can hardly hope for the Chinese people here to have confidence for future prosperity under Beijing's rule after 1997. I know I'd be worried."

Bob Broadfoot, of the private Political and Economic Risk Consultancy, put it bluntly: "What is happening in Beijing has simply crystalized the concern already felt that Hong Kong will be in a very vulnerable position. The people I have spoken to are very pessimistic. I have had Hong Kong businessmen say to me quite bluntly in the past twenty-four hours, 'Hong Kong has had it'." He added: "There is now no commerce whatsoever into China. Joint ventures, investment, all that has ground to a halt. They've all turned their backs on China. Anger is only part of it — I think there is a deep revulsion at what is going on in

China, and they want no part of it." If there was flight money already leaving Hong Kong, it is now a stampede.

Even so, as we point out in our final chapter, aside from the political events in China there have been economic reforms that are by now deeply entrenched. The forces of capitalism already unleashed may be unstoppable. Many Chinese firms, which operate similarly to Canadian Crown corporations, are increasing their investments in both Hong Kong and Canada. Owned by Chinese provinces that are determined to modernize and industrialize, these firms are not even sending their earnings back to China, but are reinvesting the profits abroad.

1/ HONG KONG: THE BOILER ROOM OF CAPITALISM

It's almost noon, halfway through the work day in frenetic Hong Kong. As it has for over a hundred years, the cast-iron cannon on the harbor's edge at North Point belonging to Jardine Matheson, the ancient British trading hong, is about to signal the event. A tall, sullen-looking employee of Jardine, dressed in a trim grey uniform, his round face topped by a fringe of greasy hair and an undersized military cap, waves a small group of British tourists away. As they prime their cameras, Jardine's man loads and fires a single blank shell. A loud crack punches out over Hong Kong's steaming, congested harbor, ricocheting past a small wooden sampan carrying two large pots of steaming soup and a single grey-haired woman, who, standing, sways to-and-fro over the stern-mounted oar. From under her wide-brimmed hat she calls out in a high voice, for all in the harbor to hear, that her soup is fresh and low-priced. The crack of the cannon reverberates through a jammed, floating suburb of teak junks. Like fifteenth-century galleons their sterns seem to rise impossibly high above the black slick that surrounds them. While adults bend to their work — fishing valuable garbage from the scummy water, operating tiny restaurants, repairing motors and rebuilding their leaky boats — wide-eyed children scamper over coils of rope and the flotsam of a scavenger's life.

Beyond the ancient junks the noise of the cannon bounces off an astounding collection of ships that carry the flags of the world's great trading nations, into this, the world's busiest harbor. So great is the flotilla that the eye cannot capture it all. Just as you think you have taken it all in, another ship appears out of the scalding haze, to create layer upon layer of ocean-going perpetual motion. Giant freighters, tended by scores of smaller ships, lie at anchor everywhere. British and American warships, their narrow swept-back decks bristling with computer-guided weaponry, stand at ease in the sun; only their rotating radar is awake and ready. Through the shifting maze on the water move thousands of seagoing commuters. Hovercraft race from harbor-side skyscrapers, carrying briefcase-toting salarymen to their homes around the island. And 420 times a day, the old green ships of the Star Ferry Company zigzag cross the harbor from the financial district, Central, on Hong Kong Island, to Kowloon on the mainland. Bearing starry names like *Meridian*, *Celestial* and *Northern*, they carry thousands of passengers daily on a winding fifteen-minute run across the harbor. Police gunboats and helicopters buzz above and through it all in a futile attempt to sort out the traffic. Only the huge, bullying freighters command enough respect to cut a straight line. Above it all, as if landing on the very deck of a superfreighter, Boeing 747s glide by-the-minute out of the burning sky to the dock-side airport.

The puff of blue smoke from Jardine's ancient gun is tossed skyward by the hot, pungent winds blowing in from the distant hills of China. It twists into a swirl above the entrance to the great traffic tunnel that runs under the harbor between Central and Kowloon, then rushes higher, brushing against some of the most spectacular architecture in the world. Jammed into impossibly small spaces the towering structures line the harbor, seeming to push and pull against one another, as if each were vying for attention. From a distance, the gleaming towers appear to be so tightly stacked that they merge into a solid wall of glass and granite that some mythical giant has built, and then draped in fantastic splashes of neon light. In the early evening, when the forty-degree heat and a mauve haze shrouds the city, the signs then seem to grow in size, blur into a surrealistic devil's-tattoo that draws the eyes of everyone on the crowded streets to a heaven filled with pulsing corporate logos.

In the corporate towers, in the boardrooms patrolled by powerful executives, where so many decisions now affecting Canada are being made, the green hills of Hong Kong Island rise sharply to Victoria Peak. Winding roads rise like goat trails up the side. And hidden away down lush green cul-de-sacs are the mansions of the rich — the higher one climbs, the more monied the occupants. Sprouting here and there, at almost impossible angles, are gleaming apartment complexes. Some are wave-shaped, following the curve of the hills, while others appear to be precariously balanced as they erupt suddenly from the steep hillside. High above the frantic congestion of the harbor and the streets of Central, young couples, their arms entangled, follow stone paths to the top of Victoria Peak, while puffing, breathless tourists turn and aim their cameras back over the harbor and beyond, to the Pearl River estuary and the blue, mist-covered mountains of the Chinese province of Guangdong.

Toiling below Victoria Peak are five and a half million people shoehorned onto 200 islands and islets spread across 1,068 square kilometres of territory running east of the Pearl River estuary to Guangdong. Smaller in area than Prince Edward Island, Hong Kong is one of the most hotly competitive environments on earth. In Central's crush, it is as if almost all the colony's five and a half million people are wedged between the office towers and the harbor. It is here that Hong Kong's reputation as the world's most stressful city becomes palpable. Here a simple ten-block walk turns into a marathon ordeal of extreme noise and sickening pollution. Emergency vehicles snarled in Central's traffic wail helplessly. Cars push through the human crush and humans push through the iron gridlock. Westerners, at least those not used to the car exhaust and extreme heat, look pale and fretful. And everywhere the constant, jagged rip of jackhammers adds to their anxiety.

This is a city that is permanently under construction. On any given day, officials estimate that work crews toil in 500 gaping wounds in its streets. Helmetless men, stripped to the waist and covered in grime and sweat, are blasting and building at every turn. At least five new hotels and office towers are under construction at any given time. Only a handful of the old colonial buildings and monuments have survived. One of the few is the Legislative Council Chamber in the heart of Central, where Themis, the Greek goddess of justice, stands mournfully alone, blackened by car exhaust. All around her mirrored towers press inexorably closer.

Nothing stands for long in this boiler room of capitalism. It is a plastic society, powered by the incalculable force of greed and the subtle panic that comes from being hemmed in by a billion people living on the razor's edge of extreme poverty. The pace is fast in Hong Kong — blazing fast. Elevator doors slam open and shut in three seconds, one-third the time usually allowed in North America. Restaurants and theatres have become mere boardroom annexes, where businessmen wheel-and-deal over portable telephones. The density of Rolls-Royces, and per-capita consumption of cognac, are the highest in the world. The stress of living in Hong Kong begins almost at birth. Even six-year-olds are forced to compete for places in the best schools.

Unlike Rome and Paris or the other great cities of the world, Hong Kong really has no memorials to a glorious past that can outshine its monuments to the present. Here diamonds, gold, money, property and, above all, power — uninhibited power, the kind that can destroy the symbols of the past on a whim and construct the future any way it wants — hold sway. After losing three historic buildings, and failing to stop a single development, the colony's Heritage Society collapsed. And now, the colony's only synagogue — a turn-of-the-century Sephardic building with sweeping marble pillars and giant buttresses — will soon be blasted to the ground. But in Greed City, what little resistance there is can be quickly overcome by an offer to build a new air-conditioned building and a promise to construct a sort of a "souvenir" replica of the old synagogue above a four-story building, a replica that critics say would be little more than a monument to Hong Kong's greed.

Blackened Themis stands dirty and now sadly alone in one of the most modern city centres in the world. Hong Kong's giant corporate offices are connected by miles of open, elevated walkways. These are lined with shops and restaurants which always seem to be jammed with crisply tailored businessmen hurrying from one boardroom to another. The city's mild climate means that the dreary closed-box design that so dominates North American architecture has been dispensed with. In Hong Kong, escalators literally sweep people off the streets and up into the open base of this skyscraper or that. In the atriums of some buildings, groups of tourists often stand with their backs arched and heads tilted back, as they marvel at the unobstructed view of the ceiling towering above them.

Although the ancient walled city near the Hong Kong International Airport is still such a dark cesspool of poverty that even the brilliant sunlight that hangs daily over the city can barely penetrate its narrow feces-smeared streets, there is hardly a beggar to be found in Central. And the only rickshaws left are piloted by wiry, yellow-toothed old men in wide straw hats who make a living posing for the tourists outside the Star Ferry terminal. Poverty, or what to the Western eye appears to be poverty, encroaches on Central only in the evening, when the inhabitants of the junks climb over the seawalls to squat on a narrow ribbon of dead grass that runs between the financial district's expressways and the harbor. Towering above them in the evening haze are the magic splashes of neon light that they cannot read but whose almost religious significance they no doubt understand.

The human crush that surges through Hong Kong's streets in search of wealth and the toys and the security that it brings is made up primarily of Cantonese Chinese, with a sprinkling of Western expatriates: British, American, Australian and increasingly Canadian. Surprisingly, a 1988 study by the Commission for Canada in Hong Kong found that as many as 38,000 Canadians may be living in the colony. This is four times the official Hong Kong administration figure, and nearly more than the numbers of Britons and Americans combined. The number of Canadians in Hong Kong is growing daily — ten Canadian babies are born each month in the city. These figures underscore an important new element of life in the booming colony that reflects more on Canada than it does on Hong Kong: thousands of new Hong Kong Canadians — people who stayed in Canada just long enough to meet the basic landed-immigrant requirements for Canadian citizenship — are returning to the city where fortunes can be built overnight. It's not that Hong Kong investors with their shiny new citizenship have not done well on this side of the Pacific — they already have an estimated $2 billion invested in Canadian manufacturing and another $6 billion in real estate — it's just, well . . . in Greed City, profits can mushroom almost instantly, and the colony's taxman (a person that new Chinese Canadians hate in this country) rarely takes a slice. And when he does, it is never more than 15 per cent.

The number of Chinese Canadians in Hong Kong and in Canada just keeps on growing and growing. About 18,000 Hong Kong students are now studying in Canada and another 50,000 to 60,000 graduates of Canadian universities are living in the colony. Every major Canadian university has an alumni association in the colony. In fact, the University of Toronto's Hong Kong alumni association claims a larger membership than the Toronto chapter of the association does.

In a fundamental way the colony still operates as it did when a tough and violent group of Britons, bent on dealing opium within China, raised the Union Jack over the island in 1847. It was created as a commercial outpost, and although the city and its economy are far more important to the world now, it remains little more than that today. While a flaccid, potbellied British administration still pretends to rule, the colony remains above all a corporate theocracy. As was the case when the colony was founded, the high priests are a select club of corporate barons who rule through the sheer (in some cases incalculable) weight of their wealth. They are worshipped because they are rich. They lead the colony because they are rich. Their every move is followed slavishly, simply because they are rich. But this surprises no one in Hong Kong. It has always been this way: a bloody, sweat-drenched blast furnace, where vast fortunes are forged with virtually no interference from government, whether it be from far-off London or the local colonial administration. So little has changed over Hong Kong's 150-year life. As the newspapers of yesteryear were, today's Hong Kong *Tattler*, a large glossy magazine, is dedicated to little else but pictures of the wealthy attending this party or that. As it was a hundred years ago, the Hong Kong and expatriate millionaires always have a beautiful and stunningly jeweled woman on their arm or riding with them in their chauffeur-driven Rolls-Royce.

The power of that corporate theocracy was never more spectacularly evident than it was on Black Monday, the day that stock markets around the world crashed, and threatened to devastate the Hong Kong Stock Exchange. On that day, headlines in media baron Rupert Murdoch's *South China Morning*

Post screamed that the colony's silver-haired, beak-nosed governor was meeting with a committee to discuss how to pull the Hong Kong Stock Exchange out of the wreckage. The governor need not have bothered. The colony's real rulers, a powerful trio of billionaires known as The Three Musketeers, who may control as much 40 per cent of all that moves on the Hong Kong Stock Exchange, had already taken action. Led by property-and-energy tycoon Li Ka-shing, the three took matters into their own hands and bought massively into the market. As if on command, the exchange turned around and pulled out of its steep decline. You see, money can fix anything in Hong Kong. And, yes, as always, the billionaire trio managed to turn a windfall profit for their trouble, while the civil administration held yet another round of meetings to discuss what the three had done.

The biggest test for Hong Kong's wealthy elite, and indeed, the colony's reason for existing in the first place, will come in 1997, when a particularly grim and utilitarian group crosses Hong Kong's harbor to worship beneath her brilliant neon firmament. In the late 1970s, the Chinese government made clear that they want their piece of booming real estate returned when Britain's lease on the property runs out in 1997. Ultimately, Britain's decision would have a far-reaching, and to date, lucrative impact on Canada, particularly in Toronto and Vancouver. In 1984, after two years of negotiations, representatives of the United Kingdom and the People's Republic of China initialled a draft agreement on the future of Hong Kong. The Chinese agreed to take the colony back as a Special Administrative Region, and promised to give it a high degree of autonomy for fifty years, in recognition of what it called Hong Kong's unique social, economic and legal status. The buzz phrase in the colony was that the Chinese had promised to operate Hong Kong as a "system within a system" well into the next century.

But the problem is that "degree of autonomy" is defined differently by each side. As a result, not everyone in Hong Kong, particularly those who have survived upheavals in China before, believes that Hong Kong's capitalist ways will remain untouched. Scores of groups, from academic associations to trade unions, have demanded that democratic institutions, such as open elections, be enshrined in a new constitution before 1997. While, from the Western point of view at least, this seems like a reasonable demand, it is viewed as a radical proposition in the East, not only in Beijing, but also in the colony's boardrooms where the billionaire proprietors want to keep spinning fortunes just as they always have. If that means supporting Beijing's opposition to even the thinnest form of limited democracy in return for the right to keep their wealth, then so be it.

One of the high priests of Greed City, the fantastically wealthy Hong Kong casino magnate Stanley Ho, is typical in his opposition. Here is a man who is taking a great interest in Canada, and yet he hates all talk of democratic reform, claiming that duplicitous politicians would, in some fashion, corrupt the colony. The inference is that corporate barons are somehow far more trustworthy and benevolent than elected representatives would be. Above all Ho believes that they can keep Hong Kong booming long after the Red Chinese army has replaced the British garrison. Along with Ho, others, like Li Ka-shing, hope to convince the Chinese that things are just fine the way they are by sitting on Beijing's committee that is overseeing the transfer of the colony. By helping to steer the communist takeover of Hong Kong, Li hopes that his empire — at least the part that he has not transferred to Canada — will be saved from the communist Chinese.

Hong Kong's wealthiest citizens have also offered billions of dollars' worth of placating gifts to Beijing's communist rulers. They have been warmly received. For instance, when billionaire shipowner Sir Yue-long Pao toured his home town of Ningho in

China, thousands of children greeted his thirty-car convoy in a beautifully choreographed display of gratitude. Despite crushing student riots in Beijing, China's pragmatic Marxist leadership under Deng Xiaoping is not only welcoming the super-capitalists home in the name of economic advancement, but is also accepting their philanthropy, which in 1987 alone helped to pay for the construction of 2,000 schools and 100 hospitals in China.

The fact that both the billionaires and communists are anxious to work together shows just how badly they want Hong Kong's traditions to remain intact. Hong Kong was created as a money-spinning venture, and this odd alliance of communists and capitalists wants it to continue spinning money. Their ideology aside, Beijing's reasons for resisting democratic reform in the colony are also ironically linked to the colony's tumultuous and violent origins. Like the first rough-hewn British businessmen who arrived and erected the colony's fabled hongs (former British-controlled companies operating in China), like the Hong Kong and Shanghai Banking Corp. and Jardine, China too wants to make a fortune in Hong Kong by using it as a foreign-currency generator. The communists see Hong Kong as a hothouse where their own officials can learn to become global businessmen — a factory sprouting state-controlled Li Kashings — who will revolutionize the communist country's economy, not only internally, but abroad, by making direct investments in foreign economies.

To that end, the Chinese, primarily through the state-controlled companies operated by its twenty-one provinces, have already launched a relentless drive to literally purchase Hong Kong. China is already the colony's largest foreign investor, accounting for 10 per cent of all activity on the Hong Kong Stock Exchange. This wave of Chinese investment has been washing over all sectors of the colony's economy for nearly five years now. And it has touched all aspects of economic life. A company operated by the southern Chinese province of Guangdong became Hong Kong's largest taxi operator in 1988 when it paid $17.4 million (Can.) for 168 cab licences. And some of Hong Kong's most spectacular investments have been made with Chinese money. CITIC, an international investment company that Beijing founded in 1979, spent $170 million in 1987 for a 12.5 per cent stake in Cathay Pacific Airways, Hong Kong's famous flag carrier. CITIC, which also purchased a 50 per cent interest in a pulp mill in Castlegar, B.C., in 1986, is also a major investor in a multimillion-dollar project to build a second tunnel under Victoria harbor, linking congested Hong Kong Island to the Kowloon peninsula.

All twenty-one of China's provincial administrations operate companies in the colony. In fact, businesses operated by provincial administrations have acquired real estate and corporations in Hong Kong that are apparently worth well over $5 billion (U.S.). But there is more at stake than merely buying companies. Fang Zheng Ping, a deputy general manager of China Everbright Holdings Co. Ltd., a major Chinese firm with sprawling operations in Hong Kong, maintains that China does not intend to throw ice water on Hong Kong's hotly capitalistic ways. On the contrary, he said that the Chinese will use the colony to modernize and internationalize their own economy, by training a new generation of corporate administrators in Central's commercial towers. And for the sake of maintaining a strong front, many Hong Kong businessmen are buying the communist business-as-usual line, arguing that in ten years Hong Kong will simply exchange one set of rulers for another. The political stripe of the new government is of little or no consequence.

But, in reality, the mood of Hong Kong's middle class is one of pronounced and growing dread. As the communists tighten their grip on Hong Kong, this dread is helping to squeeze out money and people. As a result, a human bridge is beginning to form between Canada, Hong Kong and China. As 1997 nears, an ever-deepening flood of Hong Kong money and — far more important in the long run — Hong Kong citizens, is being channeled toward Canada, both to protect old fortunes and to forge new ones. The federal government and the provinces have been making sure that only the most qualified and wealthiest parachute into Canada. And that has generated a comical, and at times, angry battle between the provinces as they fight like starving dogs over a meaty bone for their share of the wealth from the Hong Kong exodus. The battle over wealthy immigrants has become so intense that Quebec and British Columbia may offer to guarantee the viability of new investments that are built to secure Canadian passports — even agreeing to reimburse immigrants and pay off creditors if their passport-for-cash ventures fail. For provincial politicians, who believe that the wealthy immigrants can create jobs and diversify their economies, the stakes are high. Most experts believe that the vast majority of Hong Kong immigrants entering Canada under business and investor immigration categories are millionaires, with a few billionaires sprinkled in for good measure.

The answer to the question of why Canada agreed to import nearly three times as many wealthy Hong Kong residents as did the United States and Australia is not easy to find. You won't find the answer at the Commission for Canada in Hong Kong: they spend a great deal of their time trying *not* to answer that particular query. They like to point out that they don't actively seek out the rich and educated; such applicants just happen to arrive daily at the Commission's office. Of course, this is quite simply bureaucratic double-talk. The Commission's staff may argue that they don't send cars around to pick up Canada's new Chinese citizens. But they do keep a running list of investor funds that offer citizenship in return for cash (usually this translates into citizenship for real estate) and they regularly broker deals to the rich and powerful of Hong Kong through the Commission's trade group.

The real reason for the stampede to cash in on the Hong Kong exodus is hooked to the great recession of 1981-82. For example, Alberta government officials were appalled at the havoc wreaked on their energy-dependent, single-commodity economy in those years. They now see the arrival of wealthy Hong Kong residents as a way to diversify away from oil. Each rich Hong Kong immigrant, said one Alberta official, is probably worth $1 million, and he will create jobs for seven Canadians. And in true Alberta fashion he adds, "and they are never on welfare." In fact, it is not the case that the Hong Kong immigrants are all creating new jobs: most of the new immigrants entering under business categories quickly get around to investing in Canadian real estate.

An attitude similar to that of the Albertan prevails in Quebec, which, of all the provinces, has one of the most ambitious Hong Kong recruiting programs. This is despite the fact that most Hong Kong Chinese immigrants who enter Quebec quickly flee to either Vancouver or Toronto. British Columbia also obviously believes that Hong Kong immigration is the key to long-term economic growth. In 1988 it opened an office in Hong Kong to help lure students in the colony to B.C. The provincial government charges $100 a person to provide information on the province's school system and administer a number of academic tests. The three-man office hopes to attract about 300 students a year from Hong Kong, each of whom they say spends about $10,000 for housing and tuition to attend a public high school.

The number of talented Hong Kong Chinese who have left for Canada is astounding. The exodus has become so extreme that beleaguered Hong Kong companies have had to stage recruiting drives in Canada in an attempt to lure their former employees back. Some large hotels nearing completion in Hong Kong will have their openings delayed because qualified staff cannot be found. The Hong Kong and Shanghai Bank, which purchased the failing Bank of British Columbia in 1986, lost 10 per cent of its 670 officers and executives last year to emigration, and expects the exodus to grow far worse as 1997 nears. With the colony's economy ripping along at a booming 25 per cent, and unemployment running at a sliver-thin 1.6 per cent, the problem will become critical. A 1988 poll of computer-industry executives revealed that two thirds of all professionals in that sector plan to flee abroad over the next five years. And forecasts predict that as many as 100,000 people a year could leave as 1997 draws closer — and to date at least, Canada is clearly the destination of choice. While at first glance 100,000 may not appear to be a high figure, it becomes astronomical when placed against the fact that Hong Kong's educated middle class accounts for less than a third of its population.

Clearly the exodus from Hong Kong will grow. In 1987, Canada issued 22,000 immigrant visas to Hong Kong citizens. By comparison, the United States issued 8,517 visas in 1987 and Australia 8,000. Already almost 700,000 (and, by some estimates, perhaps as many as a million) Chinese, primarily from Hong Kong, already call Canada home. While many people in Vancouver remain true to their lumberjack roots and complain bitterly about the influx of Hong Kong cash and people, Toronto is quietly displacing New York City as the municipality with the largest Chinese population in North America. And incredibly, the phenomenon is just beginning. Each working day, in their offices overlooking Hong Kong harbor, the Canadian Commission hands out about 400 visa applications and more and more of those will be accepted as 1997 nears.

When asked why they are leaving their vibrant, hard-driving community to confront cold weather and growing racial tensions in Canada, Chinese immigrant parents invariably answer: "It is because of 1997. I am not worried, but it's for my children." These doubts remain despite assurances, from Beijing and the colony's corporate leaders, that Hong Kong will continue to operate as a system-within-a-system. But after the riots Beijing there is obviously little faith that the system will be left intact. And even if it is, many other Hong Kong Chinese say that they believe Hong Kong's economy will be destroyed because it will become like China's: a bureaucratic puzzle that rarely produces effective economic decisions. According to Hong Kong political scientist Joseph Cheng: "People know that democracy simply isn't on. The choice now is to emigrate or, if they can't, stay quiet and keep their fingers crossed."

Their worries are anchored deep in the colony's past. Lord Napier — nicknamed "laboriously vile" by the Chinese — ripped Hong Kong from the Asian giant's southern flank after he defeated China in the 1839-42 Opium War. The Chinese never forgot, and even today, Caucasians are rarely invited into a Hong Kong Chinese home. Many of Hong Kong's richest and most successful citizens cannot speak English, the language of the *queillos* (foreign devils). Most residents can remember that just twenty-eight years ago, in 1962, China tried to topple the colony's administration by sending a wave of 70,000 refugees into Hong Kong. And then, a mere five years later, in 1967, loudspeakers outside the communist Bank of China building, in the heart of Central, called on all Hong Kong residents to shake off the yoke of imperialism and overthrow their British rulers. Rioters, led by Mao's Red Guards, shook the colony for six months before the British army, using brute force, was finally able to restore order. And then there was the body count. Each day Hong Kong officials counted the number of bodies floating down the Pearl River to measure the violence in Mao's China.

Faith in Beijing's ability to govern Hong Kong is also being buffeted by shifting economic fortunes China. As part of the reforms undertaken after 1980, the central Chinese government loosened its grip on the country's economy by moving some of the responsibility for economic planning to individual provinces. But the competition between the Asian giant's twenty-one provinces has led to deficits and inflation, and to what some analysts in Hong Kong describe as "economic warlordism," a reference to a period earlier in this century when Chinese strongmen and their armies competed for control of China. In fact, competition between the Chinese provinces has become acute. Increasingly their struggles are waged by expanding state-controlled firms into Hong Kong, where provincial bureaucrats can acquire a life-style unavailable to them at home. Indeed, the Chinese government lost track of how many state-run companies operate in Hong Kong, and has launched a drive to count them. Increasingly both the Chinese Communist Party and the central-government authorities appear unable to bring warring provincial authorities to heel. There are even reports of trade wars raging between provinces. Other provinces are balking at Beijing's attempts, by the arbitrary allocation of the country's scarce resources, to bring inflation under control. In one instance involving raw silk, a highly profitable commodity, local government officials sent troops to patrol provincial borders and prevent their silkworm cocoons being transported to other localities. The problem has become especially acute in prosperous Guangdong. This province, which surrounds Hong Kong and is increasingly seen as the colony's cheap labor factory, seems more intent on following Hong Kong's lead than Beijing's.

The inhabitants of Hong Kong live next door to a nation of just over a billion people who could easily tumble backward into severe poverty and demand an end to capitalism on its territory. The pressure exerted by China's huge presence is not lost on Hong Kong's wealthy middle class. Combined with what many China-watchers say is the inability of Chinese rulers to accept any kind of democratic reforms, and the increasing suspicion that the British intend to sell out the colony by blocking attempts to erect a democratic bridgehead in China, this pressure leaves many people looking to Canada for sanctuary.

If you are a particularly nervous Hong Kong Chinese businessman, you can buy insurance in the form of a Canadian passport for the price of cheap Toronto condominium. By investing as little as $150,000 in a Canadian-based venture-capital fund, you can secure landed-immigrant status, and eventually, citizenship. Other Hong Kong businessmen actually create new manufacturing and other ventures in Canada, in return for citizenship, and so acquire protection from any future fickleness on the part of Hong Kong's rulers.

So, as the colony's big-money men and wealthy middle class build a hedge against a possible change in thinking in Beijing, which might suddenly find people such as Li Ka-shing and Stanley Ho incompatible with communism, Canada is growing richer by the day. By moving assets to Canada, assets usually administered by family members who are becoming Canadians, Hong Kong fortunes will be protected to a degree. And as the big players, like Li and Ho, bet against the house, thousands of lesser residents of Hong Kong, but millionaires nonetheless, have taken note and are imitating their corporate heroes. As a result, forty-five years after Li Ka-shing, and thousands like him, followed their parents and grandparents out of China to the safety of Hong Kong, they are again fleeing communism. This time their flight usually takes them to Canada, the United States and Australia. Their arrival in the West has had a profound, growing, and above all, positive effect on Canada. True, their arrival in Canada bothered a handful of backward newspaper columnists in Vancouver. And the tired remnants of the old British community in the city complain that the wave of Chinese people and money lapping against the Pacific coast is eroding the city's WASP character. This is odd, because over the last year, both U.S. companies and Fletcher Challenge, the giant New Zealand-based multinational, have bought up vast pieces of the province's pulp and paper and lumber industry. Although nothing matters more than forestry in the B.C. economy, nothing has been written about these buyouts. Many economists, meanwhile, argue that the flow of Asian money into the city is about the only good thing to happen to Vancouver following the western commodities bust of 1981.

Ultimately, the influx of Hong Kong money and people will benefit Canada, but the impact will not be fully appreciated until the first decade of the next century. Consider, for example, the implications of the fact that Canada's top universities now find themselves inundated with applications from Hong Kong's brightest students. Most of these aggressive young people who, unlike the majority of Canada's top students, prefer to study business and science rather than the arts, will exit from Canadian schools, not only with a degree, but with Canadian citizenship either assured, or easily within their grasp. Not only are these students the youngest generation of the cream of Hong Kong society, but in many cases they are the spearhead of their families' fortunes, which they will carry across the Pacific to Canada. It becomes their responsibility to protect and expand the family's wealth in Canada.

By 1988, students from Hong Kong accounted for a full quarter of all foreign students studying in Canada. That fact is not lost on Canada's largest post-secondary institution, the University of Toronto. University President George Connell says that the influx of students has actually pushed the level of academic achievement up, and will ultimately improve Canada's science and engineering community. According to Connell: "They are a very visable presence and they are consistently high achievers." Of course, Canada's cash-starved universities have other reasons to benefit from 1997. The University of Toronto has already awarded an honorary doctorate to Hong Kong real estate billionaire Cheng Yu-tung for his massive financial contributions to the school, and Connell has traveled to Hong Kong to talk to alumni, students and potential investors.

Behind the big players is a supporting cast of smaller investors. They are rebuilding Canada's fashion industry at a time when most people in that industry feel that the Canada-U.S. Free Trade agreement will destroy it. Others are using their expertise in electronics to spin off companies here and still others are moving their families here while they fly between the two countries. If the worst comes about in 1997, they will be able to save at least part of their families' holdings, which more often than not amount to millions of dollars.

Imagine the positive implications for Canada when wealthy Hong Kong families, who have expanded and anchored their corporate command centres in Canada and Hong Kong, push deeper and deeper into the Chinese market. Imagine the payoff for this country from a Chinese community of one and a half million people which retains strong links to China, a country they have a deep attachment to, and badly want to see prosper. These passionate capitalists (they have an abiding hate for Canada's initiative-destroying tax system) are playing a role in another revolution, one that involves the transformation of mainland China into a major industrialized country. Corporate barons like Li Ka-shing, and smaller Canadian firms led by people such as Toronto computer-whiz James Ting, the Shanghai-born, Canadian-educated head of International Semi-Tech Microelectronics Inc., have already broken into China, Ting signing unique, three-way computer high-tech assembly and development agreements with firms in Hong Kong, China and Canada.

Canada has had for some time a huge trade surplus with the People's Republic of China because of the Asian giant's appetite for wheat, wood pulp, rubber and plastic materials. Increasingly, though, mainland China is becoming an active participant in the Canadian economy as it searches for expertise, new markets, raw materials and much-needed foreign currency. Until recently, most mainland Chinese enterprises took the form of joint ventures with established firms familiar with the North America market. Now, China, either through its own state-owned corporations, or indirectly through Hong Kong's aggressive capitalists, is pouring millions into everything from fox-breeding farms and ginseng soft-drink factories to Chinese clothing and furniture outlets. Natural resource projects are the big draw for the simple reason that China wants to tie down secure, long-term supplies of pulp, petrochemicals, coal and potash. These novice capitalists have also learned from Hong Kong's entrepreneurs and are speculating on commercial and residential real estate in the volatile Toronto and Vancouver markets. Ultimately, this link through Hong Kong to China may be the single biggest advantage Canadians gain from the wave of immigration and the flight of money from the Asian colony.

2/ LI KA-SHING: THE NEW *TAIPAN*

Li Ka-shing's bodyguard is nervous. Dressed in an oversized dark-blue suit, wearing the face of a smiling Buddha on the body of a linebacker, he shifts with a slight to-and-fro motion away from his favorite observation post behind a large fern. Three receptionists, all seemingly identical in height and wearing trim blazers, and dozens of employees, their desks surrounded by models of apartment projects that Li is building in Hong Kong, have also taken note. There is a bit of commotion at the bottom of a sweeping staircase that leads up to Li's penthouse office — the terminus of an extraordinary international operation that is slowly being transferred to Canada. And just in case there's trouble, the boss's muscle, looking a lot like the hat-tossing assassin Odd-job in the James Bond thriller *Goldfinger*, wants a closer look. He need not have bothered. The young, red-faced Canadian businessman, who wants desperately to see the fabled Li, known popularly around Hong Kong as "K.S.," or "Mr. Money," has already been turned back by Li's first line of a defence, his hellishly tough corporate secretary, Ezra Kwok.

She, slim and attractive, her face framed in a blunt corporate haircut, has pounded him into retreat by slowly repeating her mantra of denial: "I'm sorry, Mr. Li is very busy. Perhaps the next time you are in Hong Kong."

To the retreating executive the stairs seem to disappear into the ceiling. But at their top, behind automatic glass doors, down a short granite-lined hallway, in rooms appointed with Chinese antiques, Li, unaware of the commotion below, is bent over his desk. His slim, still-athletic body is wrapped as usual in a navy-blue suit, white shirt and perfectly knotted, striped tie. His expressionless mouth and sharp brown eyes are accented by arching eyebrows that poke above his black-rimmed glasses. But behind the calm face that Li seems always to present to the *queillos* (foreign devils) there is a mercurial, almost merry personality, a temperament toughened by the poverty of his youth and fired by his spectacular fortune.

This is a complicated man. Li will obligingly place his hands on a large globe and bend forward in the pose of a corporate baron for photographers trying to put the tycoon's burgeoning empire into perspective. And yet he eschews Hong Kong's standard issue diamond-studded Rolexes for his simple Seiko. He lives in the same modest seaside mansion with his wife, Amy, that he bought two decades ago, and his only nod to Western taste appears to be his love of golf, a game that he tries to play once a month. Says Li, with a shy, and strangely disarming smile for someone so powerful: "But I'm not very good." He can be moved to embarrassment by little things, like the compact disc player that his son Victor has installed crudely in the back of the front seat of the family's wine-colored Rolls-Royce. "My son had it put in," says Li, leaving his passenger to wonder why one of the world's richest men would bother to explain.

He is also unassuming, gregarious and carefree enough about his own security to offer a stranger a ride downtown through snarled traffic from the Hong Kong International Airport. He even holds the trunk lid open for his unknown guest, while his driver remains seated complacently behind the steering wheel. Later, sitting bolt upright in his Rolls, he expresses exaggerated concern about the car's poor air-conditioning, and his passenger's accommodations, and insists on phoning ahead to make sure a room is available at the Hong Kong Hilton. Of course, he just happens to own the prestigious address, one of the top hotels in the world.

While the Canadian businessman is riding the elevator back down into Hong Kong's financial district, Li is being briefed on things Canadian. Over the last twenty-five years, Canada has taken up more and more of the tycoon's time, as he moves some of his assets — and more importantly his family — away from Beijing's rapidly tightening fist. The Canadian Imperial Bank of Commerce (CIBC), which wanted to expand its base of operations in Hong Kong and China, first befriended Li in a troublesome property deal some twenty years ago. Later, the bank even loaned him a top manager when some of Li's own executives mutinied. The big Canadian bank and Li have become good friends and each has used the other in the advancement of corporate goals. Not only has the CIBC ushered Li into the Canadian corporate spotlight by helping him to swallow Husky Oil of Calgary and a vast chunk of Vancouver, but it has also used its connection to Li to help tap a wave of Hong Kong flight money with investment pools that can ultimately lead to Canadian citizenship. The CIBC, blessed by its connection with Li, has seen its Asian business boom. More and more wealthy Hong Kong residents inquire at the CIBC offices in the colony, located conveniently just below Li's penthouse perch, about moving their assets to Canada.

Now, hardly a day goes by when Li does not hear from his Canadian operation or face questions about his Canadian dealings from the colony's aggressive press and increasingly worried administration. Their main query is always the same. It is the one that most residents of Hong Kong want answered: Does Li intend to move the headquarters of his far-flung operation to

Canada? While Li consistently denies that this is his intention, the fact that both his sons have taken out Canadian citizenship suggests to many people in the colony that he is doing just that. Other Hong Kong multibillionaires, such as gambling magnate Stanley Ho, and jewelry czar Cheng Yu-tung, have also taken note, and are either engaged in joint ventures directly with Li in Canada, or are striking out on their own to find out what Li, the colony's leading citizen, finds so intriguing about Canada. As they do, dozens of lesser billionaires and thousands of millionaires from Hong Kong are following in their wake to Canada.

Li's Canadian operation grows almost daily. His second-oldest son, Victor, now twenty-four, stepped out from his father's shadow to head the firm building the $8-billion Pacific Place, a so-called mini Manhattan to be built on the now-vacant Expo 86 grounds on Vancouver's False Creek. Li says that he is considering adding to the energy holdings in Canada, which he beefed up with the acquisition of Canterra Energy of Calgary in July 1988 for just over $300 million. And Nova Corporation chairman, Robert Blair, is believed to have at one point lobbied hard to have Husky Oil, the Calgary-based oil and gas giant that is partly owned by Nova, and controlled by Li, purchase Texaco Canada from its U.S. parent. It was rumored that Li also traded heavily in Polysar Ltd. shares in 1988 when Blair waged a pitched year-long battle for the company.

Hardly a week goes by when Li does not entertain a Canadian businessman, trade official or provincial premier in his penthouse office. They all want Li to make yet another Canadian investment. Some of their proposals, it seems, do not sit well with Li. It is widely rumored in Hong Kong that the scrupulous businessman once asked a provincial premier and his executive assistant to leave his office when the politician proposed a deal to build a gambling casino in Canada. Li apparently considered that the proposal was corrupt or at least that it would damage the image he is working so hard to create in Canada.

All this activity has made Li wildly popular with Canadians in Hong Kong. In 1987 he was inducted into the Hong Kong Canadian Club. Federal and provincial trade officials in the colony virtually worship him. They regularly broker deals to the tycoon, offering him everything from Canada grocery store chains to real estate, and then they wait, like nervous brides for the gatekeeper, Ezra Kwok, to call and invite them up that arched staircase to Li's office. But the call rarely comes.

Canadian trade officials are clearly mesmerized by Li's wealth. His portrait, actually a framed copy of a *Maclean's* magazine cover, overlooks acres of deep, velvety pile in the palatial offices of the Quebec consulate in the British colony. The portrait's owner, a young Montrealer who is an investment counselor for the province, expresses typical reverence as he sits beneath the photo and gushes praise for Li: "He's a hero of mine." The counselor — his brown eyes beaming like those of a young hockey fan recalling his first face-to-face meeting with skating greatness — wants, as does every Canadian investment official in Hong Kong, the great industrialist to buy a piece of his province — anything, perhaps just a mansion in Mount Royal, a pulp mill, or a string of restaurants. If Li would only do so, then Quebec would become a legitimate part of the tycoon's booming Canadian empire, and that would focus the attention of Hong Kong's lesser stars on Canada's French-speaking province. Then, in theory at least, the economic benefits would start to roll in.

The investment official paints his latest encounter with Li in the blushed-out red tones of a teenage girl recalling her first kiss: "We met last week at the Canadian Club, and we talked."

Talking to and about Li — if there is a name Canadians love to drop in Hong Kong, it is Li's — is something Quebec officials, and all other federal and provincial investment officials from Canada, love to do. Some, like Manitoba's representative, have located their offices directly under the tycoon's penthouse perch in China House. As if acting on the advice of a *feng-shui* master who has expanded his skills to embrace the immigration business, they find themselves a few floors below Li, and just behind Hong Kong's important and always-bustling, twin-towered Exchange Square. When Canadian trade and immigration officials talk about Li their features soften, and wispy smiles cross their faces. Some are so overcome that they seem to feel the need to strike a pose. And, like rich, aging *taipans* reflecting on their own empires to younger heirs, they often stand to discuss the subject. Eventually they become reflective: they cross their arms behind their backs, knot their hands under their chins or gaze out over the harbor (nearly every Canadian federal and provincial office in the colony seems to command a magnificent view of Hong Kong harbor). They imagine that somehow, through their association with Li, they can tap the incredible bounty beneath their windows and transfer it, giant container ship and tiny teak junk, to Canada. Finally, after a long pause, they speak, but usually they have little to say, because Li, the son of Chinese refugees who truly started with nothing, hedges his bets and tells the *queillos* little. "Oh, I've met him many times," says Alberta representative Jack Kennedy, a tall, craggy Calgary lawyer and long-time Alberta Conservative. "He's a wonderful man." But then, such clipped sentences about Li are followed by longer pauses, and if-only-you-knew-what-I-know facial expressions, and a conversation about the vast potential in Hong Kong immigration — always the vast potential — but little more about Li.

They can hardly be blamed for their enthusiasm. Li, thanks to the generosity and forward-thinking strategy of the Hong Kong and Shanghai Banking Corp., is the richest Chinese businessman in the colony — *Fortune* magazine ranks his fortune in the $14 billion (U.S.) range — and one of the first to look West to expand beyond the colony's borders. As a result, he shows three faces or masks to the world: to the East and Beijing he stands for stability and continued investment in the colony, during a time of grave doubt; in the old British territory itself, where investors watch his every move, he must be seen to extend his roots deeper and deeper into Hong Kong's booming economy (to cut and run would cause a hemorrhage of flight capital and shatter the colony's future); and to the West, particularly Canada, he stands for quick economic diversification and a new source of financing, capable of injecting vast amounts of wealth into the country. To the third face have been drawn premiers, scores of businessmen and federal and provincial civil servants.

Li rotates his masks constantly. He sits on Beijing's committee to establish the rules of government that will come into effect following the colony's transfer to China. To name just a couple of dozens of Li's business ventures in China: he is attempting to accelerate the Asian giant's fledgling space industry by launching a communications satellite on the tip of a Chinese rocket; his giant hong, Hutchinson Whampoa Ltd., has entered a three-way deal with British Telecom and the Peking-controlled China International Trust and Investment Corporation to build a cable TV network in the colony, and perhaps satellite TV beyond that. Many of these projects are designed to span 1997 because, says Li, if Hong Kong remains useful to China its super-charged economy will be left intact.

To help ensure that China continues to let the colony follow its competitive course, Li is consolidating his corporate wealth on the Hong Kong Stock Exchange, and cementing confidence in the colony's future, by financing some $25 billion in new investments in massive projects such as a second international airport in Hong Kong. And increasingly, he shows the third Mask internationally. By doing so he hopes that he can convince Beijing that it would be simply too embarrassing to bring down such a world-renowned businessman. To that end, on one visit to London in 1988, he lunched with Prime Minister Margaret Thatcher, was photographed with Princess Alexandra at a Chinese festival in London and even had his lieutenant in the House of Lords denounce proposed democratic reforms in the colony. But most of the time, when Li sits alone atop China House in his antique-filled office and dons his third Mask and looks beyond Hong Kong, perhaps because of that early bailout by the CIBC, he sees Canada: "I will be retired in 1997, but both sons, they will be in charge. They will be Canadian."

Li regularly flies to Beijing and invests, both personally and corporately, at every opportunity in China. Li, who clearly has an insider's view of the looming takeover, and likely could not say otherwise, maintains that Hong Kong will continue to grow and prosper under Chinese rule: "There will be a system within a system." But then, like any street-wise investor, Li has hedged his bullish position on Hong Kong by spreading the risk. To do so requires that he endure criticism in Hong Kong as he moves some of his assets abroad. To that end, his sons Victor and Robert are working in Vancouver and Toronto where they are supervising the smooth transfer of part of the family fortune to Canada. "I admire him," says Jardine's former *taipan*, and long-time business adversary of Li, Simon Keswick. "He's an extraordinarily clever man, but he is able to benefit from the dual standards in Hong Kong for Chinese and *queillo* businessmen."

Li cultivates and capitalizes on that dual standard at every chance. He showers millions of dollars in donations on China to build schools and hospitals. More importantly, a long-term tenet of Li's strategy seems to be an assumption that Beijing can be kept at bay after 1997 if convinced that the colony's largest firms intend to stay, and that it would not only be lucrative if they did, but that it would also help China meet its own need to diversify economically. In November, 1988, Li demonstrated his resolve by joining forces with the Chinese state firm, China Resources, to build a massive residential development in Hong Kong that will not be completed until after the 1997 takeover. The so-called Tin Shui Wai development will contain 952,000 square metres of residential accommodation and 75,000 square metres of commercial facilities. Just to make sure that Beijing benefits from the deal, Li's flagship developer, Cheung Kong, guarantees China Resource's financial return on the project. As well, two other leading Chinese firms, China International Trust and Investment Corporation and China Civil Engineering Corporation, have agreed to enter a joint venture with Li in a number of spectacular projects that will also span 1997.

As part of the strategy of being in both camps at once, Li usually speaks only Cantonese at press conferences in the colony, and he is always readily accessible to Hong Kong's Chinese press. Perhaps he realizes that he can speak to Beijing's masters directly through the Cantonese-language papers. In any case, the swashbuckling capitalist in him is happy to indulge the Chinese media's craving for news of his latest real estate or corporate triumph, especially if it involves a victory over the *queillos*. Li is much more taciturn with the Western media. The authors of this book are among only a small number of Westerners who have ever interviewed the tycoon at length. In return for his no doubt careful attention, the Chinese press accords Li almost as much support as any well-paid publicist would. As a result, in the Chinese press, Li is depicted as the five-star general who led the successful and humiliating assault on the British dominance of Hong Kong's commercial life. He smashed Hong Kong Land, the colony's high-flying property company, with his cunning and his daring property deals. But his most important victory came when the Hong Kong Bank surrended Hutchinson. All this plays wonderfully in Beijing where China's leaders would no doubt rather deal with a native son than an aging white *taipan*.

The tycoon's relationship to Canada stretches back to the Second World War beyond a row of ghostly concrete bunkers high in the hills behind Kowloon near the Chinese border, to one of the most tragic periods in Canada's history. In September, 1941, Sir Winston Churchill's wartime government asked Canada to send two battalions to reinforce the British garrison at Hong Kong. A troop train was soon crossing the Canadian prairies, collecting the teenage sons of Canadian farmers. When they finally arrived in Hong Kong, most were carrying only their sidearms — the ship carrying their heavy weapons had been torpedoed by the Japanese navy. They were hopelessly outgunned, and the bunkers they defended were quickly overrun. The Canadians were routed, and the Hong Kong garrison captured. Of the 1,200 Canadians who arrived in Hong Kong only 400 survived. Many were brutally tortured to death.

During this period, Chinese refugees also streamed into the British colony by the thousands, fleeing the havoc of internal revolution and their own three-year-old war with Japan. Among those seeking a chance for a fresh start was the Li family from Chui Chow in Guangdong province in southern China. Just two years later, the father of the family, a teacher, died, leaving thirteen-year-old Li Ka-shing to care for his mother and younger brother and sister. Li found a job with a company manufacturing plastic toys and watchbands. He soon rose to the position of junior salesman, a feat he achieved by pitching sales during the day and working in the plant by night. Whenever he could spare some time — and that was seldom — he studied on his own, and true to his father's wishes he successfully completed the examination for a high school diploma. His intention was to continue his studies, but instead he was promoted again, at age twenty, to the post of general manager of the factory. By twenty-three, even while supporting his family, he had managed to save about $2,000. Just a decade after arriving in Hong Kong, in 1950, Li used those savings to finance his own plastics manufacturing business, and what has since become a multibillion-dollar empire was born. Li Ka-shing now oversees a broad range of private and public companies. His original plastics business has evolved into his flagship company, Cheung Kong (Holdings) Ltd. "Cheung Kong" means "long river" in Cantonese, an obvious reference to the Yangtze. Mainly a property developer,

Cheung Kong has direct and indirect holdings in such huge companies as Hutchinson Whampoa Ltd., Hong Kong Electric Holdings Ltd. and Green Island Cement Co. Ltd., which in turn have interests in shipping, energy, communications, retailing and construction. Together they generate annual profits in the range of $1 billion.

Although Li's incredible wealth, power and elite position in Hong Kong and Asia now give him an air of invincibility, it was not always so. The young man from Chui Chow had to battle his way up through Hong Kong's back streets into the monied elite. The members of that elite, predominantly Shanghainese textile, shipping and property entrepreneurs, tended to view Li, from their golden perches on the steep green hills above Hong Kong, as an upstart plastics salesman who might be making a lot of money, but who would never earn enough to guarantee position, prestige and that most important commodity of all in the colony, power. How wrong the old merchant families were! In a little more than a decade, Li became not only their corporate leader, but also their Churchill and king, a man whose every move must be watched, weighed, analysed and — above all — duplicated. That fact alone is why so much money is flowing from Hong Kong to Canada: the king bestowed his blessing on Canada by investing here, and now Hong Kong's lesser billionaires and millionaires are buying up the country with abandon. They are filling Canadian vaults with everything from bearer bonds to platinum watches, because what is good for the always bullish Ka-shing must obviously be good for lesser mortals, too.

To get the attention of the Shanghainese billionaires, and to star in one of the most competitive environments on earth, Li would have to gamble where other property developers passed on the play, or simply fled in panic. Li's gambit to riches was to trade tracts of prime real estate property the way some people trade precious commodities. As part of his strategy, he took what was then a revolutionary step for Hong Kong, and joint-ventured property developments with the old *queillo* companies. This was something that most of the venerable Shanghainese families, many of whom could not even speak English, had always been loath to do. But Li, who had taught himself English, and who foresaw Beijing's rising desire to have her stolen territory returned, began dealing with the colony's Caucasian corporate barons. Li handled the planning, construction, marketing and financing of huge real estate developments, but to build a buffer against risk, he pre-sold the developments to others; as often as not, to the old British hongs. It was during this period that Li cemented his contacts with the Canadian Imperial Bank of Commerce. Today, with holdings estimated at 10 per cent, he is believed to be the bank's largest individual shareholder. But says Li with a mischievious tone: "I have not said how much."

In Hong Kong's exploding property market of the late 1970s, Li's strategy proved wildly profitable. And while other wealthy real estate tycoons in the colony, like Lee Shau-kee, of Henderson Land (an associate investor in Li's Expo 86 land deal who is now also a partner in a major real estate development in Toronto) mostly built residential apartment blocks, Li started developing spectacular commercial projects. As the roaring 1970s boomed on, Li remained primarily a property developer, albeit a hugely successful one. But in the eyes of Hong Kong's rich and powerful, he was still the refugee from Chui Chow.

That perception was about to change. As Li rose and rose in Hong Kong, his reputation for spectacular luck, a reputation Vancouver's as yet innocent residents would later indirectly add to, spread far and wide. That reputation soared to new heights on January 25, 1979, the day Li vaulted from the ranks of wealthy property developers to become the colony's first Chinese *taipan*. On that cool, sunny Hong Kong day, everything seemed normal in the city: the teak junks moved among the big ocean-going ships in the harbor; the ferries carrying thousands of office workers docked, one-after-another, at the foot of the financial district; and the morning air was already thick with car exhaust and industrial smoke. Hardly anyone was aware that the crumbling barriers between Hong Kong's *queillo* and Chinese business communities were about to be blasted to the ground by Michael Sandberg.

As chairman of the Hong Kong and Shanghai Banking Corp., one of Hong Kong's oldest British firms or hongs, Sandberg sold Li the bank's 22 per cent controlling interest in Hutchinson Whampoa, the famous Hong Kong property and trading hong. If Li was in fact lucky by nature, then his luck was working overtime. Li purchased, or perhaps more accurately was given, the shares at half their net asset value. To top that, they came on a two-year deferred payment plan! Even more astounding: while the bank was keenly aware of the shares' true worth, Sandberg, as Hutchinson's then-managing director William Wyllie noted, did not give any of Li's competitors a chance, at least not a formal chance, to duel with the tycoon for the spectacular prize. Perhaps the reason was that Sandberg had also sniffed the winds blowing in from China, and had sensed a change and new tension in air. Not since the 1960s, when Mao Tse-tung's Red Guards rioted in the colony, had Beijing watched activities there so closely. And Sandberg apparently believed strongly, and wisely as it turned out, that the bank needed to enlarge the commercial role played by the Cantonese in Hong Kong. After all, despite the strong British, Canadian and American presence, it is still above all else, a Cantonese Chinese city. Placing a prominent Cantonese at the head of the colony's corporate table would send a clear signal to Beijing: the present-day captains of the old British hongs, that were so ruthlessly erected on China's southern flank, now recognize that time was running out — and quickly. The *queillos* would, and must, step aside.

This scenario seems all the more likely because the deal that propelled Li from real estate tycoon to corporate baron was pulled off even though the giant, and often jealous Hong Kong trading hongs, Jardine Matheson and Swire Pacific, as well as British entrepreneur Sir James Goldsmith, Hutchinson's management and a number of U.S. companies, were all drooling over Hutchinson. And little wonder. Hutchinson was founded in the 1840s and is the jewel of all the old hongs. Its operations touch almost every aspect of life in the colony. Indeed, it's hard to spend a dime in Hong Kong without contributing to the company's diverse earning base which includes: food, shipping, electricity and television, and more recently, oil and gas through Li's purchase of Husky. Even more telling is the fact that Li captured the biggest prize of his career at a Hong Kong and Shanghai Banking Corp. board meeting during which the leather-bound chairs, usually occupied by management representatives, Jardine and Swire, sat ominously, and hugely empty. Into the vacuum stepped Li. Beijing noticed. Hong Kong suddenly changed forever.

The Hutchinson buyout would prove critical for Li, but then he was always lucky — oh, so lucky! Just three years later, during those long and depressing months of 1982-84, when the worldwide recession and deep pessimism over the future of the colony, were cutting deeper each day into the value of Li's real estate holdings, he was able to draw on Hutchinson's deep pools of cash to support his main holding company, Cheung Kong, the vault containing most of the Li's personal wealth. As well, Hutchinson would emerge as Li's main weapon in his corporate assault on Canada. It is a name that Canadians will hear and read about more as the wash of Hong Kong money increases, and 1997 draws nearer.

One of the most important factors propelling Li in his rise to wealth was his decision to learn English. Li usually speaks to Westerners in clipped, halting sentences, but some veteran Li-watchers claim he actually has an excellent command of the language. And, while Hong Kong billionaires like Cheng Yu-tung (who is also a partner of Li's in the Expo site deal, and who is now shopping for a trust company in Canada) looked inward, Li used his hard-won skills in English to befriend the colony's Caucasian corporate barons. He shrewdly tapped the white businesses in the colony for management stars who could straddle the gap between his Chinese world and the colony's *queillo*-dominated boardrooms. Today, Li's corporate secretary, the tall, patrician George Magnus, who helped to introduce Li formally to Canada's business elite in Robert Blair's soaring, gold-capped Husky complex in Calgary, is virtually always present when the family makes a corporate move on Canada. And while Magnus remains icily detached, Hutchinson Whampoa's group secretary Simon Murray, a short, athletic, former member of the French Foreign Legion, is friendly — at least on the surface — and outgoing. Both men are ferocious in their loyalty to Li.

Even while he was dazzling China with his philanthropy and bold corporate thrusts, Li was planning a spectacular entrance into Canada. It would take place in the atrium of Bob Blair's granite-covered skyscraper. Blair, who describes Li as "builder," was one of the first Canadian businessmen to recognize that Asia, and specifically Hong Kong, could be the source of critical financing that would free the Canadian energy sector from its traditional dependence on Toronto's flaccid bankers. Blair spent years cultivating contacts in Hong Kong and China through Nova's office in the colony, which is headed by the firm's vice-president, Norma Kwok. Kwok moves easily, both socially and professionally, through Hong Kong's business world, and seems to be constantly on the move in Asia. And that is important, because unlike Canada's highly structured business environment, deals in the East are often struck on an informal basis, with a handshake. Kwok is the forerunner of a new breed of Hong Kong entrepreneur, one that seems destined to spend a large part of their careers marrying Hong Kong billionaires and millionaires to Canadian projects.

Kwok readily accepts the credit for bringing Li and Blair together in the Husky deal. But she was aided by the fact that the buy meshed with both Li's and Blair's long-term goals: Li was able to invest some of his fabulous wealth safely abroad; and Blair was able to inject new cash into Husky even as the pall of recession still shrouded Calgary's oil towers. As well, and perhaps more importantly Blair, Nova's founder and mastermind, was able to raise millions for new projects without adding to Husky's long-term debt. Says Blair: "I believe that there will be more financing coming out of Asia to Canada than there has been historically from the United States." If his Husky deal is an example of what is to come, then Blair just might be right.

Li's strategy in the Husky deal is also revealing. It dramatically underscores how ever-increasing amounts of Hong Kong money will flow to Canada through family connections in the closely knit Chinese world, and how some of Canada's largest financial houses may supply critical help. Both of Li's sons, Victor and Robert, are, as previously noted, Canadian citizens. Whether Li had his sons pursue Canadian citizenship as part of a long-range corporate strategy is open to question. Those who say their citizenship goals are driven more by business than love of Canada, argue that they could just as easily have become citizens of another country, or stayed in Hong Kong. Whatever their reasons, a very important issue for Canadians is clear: when Li Ka-shing retires, Hong Kong's leading hong, with its roots deep in China and Canada, will end up in the hands of Victor and Robert. These two young men, who enjoy skiing at Whistler and listening to their compact disc player while touring Hong Kong in their chauffeur-driven Rolls-Royce, will end up owning almost one third of downtown Vancouver, some of the country's top hotels and a giant slice of the nation's energy sector, and according to their father, possibly even a grocery store chain or two. Ultimately, they will have to decide whether they will become so-called Hong Kong astronauts, operating from corporate bases in both countries, or whether they will manage Cheung Kong and Hutchinson from Canada. What-ever happens, the pair's mere presence in Canada is already drawing a flood of money to this country.

While only the long-term future, particularly what China decides to do with Hong Kong, will determine the answer to that question, Li clearly revealed his short-term strategy when he used Victor's Canadian citizenship for leverage to escape foreign-ownership requirements in the Husky deal. And once again, as part of that game plan, he involved his old pals at the Canadian Imperial Bank of Commerce. In all, under the terms of the deal, the Li family and related corporate interests paid almost $400 million for 52 per cent of Husky. Li's Calgary-based company Union Faith (which is operated by Hutchinson) took 43 per cent of Husky and Victor Li took 9 per cent, giving the family 52 per cent of the company. The CIBC, which is always ready to oil the wheels of the cart when Li is shopping in Canada, acquired another 5 per cent. By using Victor's Cana-dian citizenship, Li was able to circumvent official Canadian government policy which opposed the sale of "financially healthy" energy companies to foreigners.

The Husky deal also marked Li's formal introduction to Canada's business elite. When Li signed the deal to take Husky, it is rumored that he told the members of his staff that, unlike Hong Kong, where his every move generates headlines, he was receiving little or no recognition in Canada. The word went out, and Blair engineered a glittering reception for Li and his son Victor. The pair stood with Blair at the top of a bank of escalators, where they greeted hundreds of corporate blue bloods with polite bows that seemed to draw a similar response from their beefy Canadian counterparts. Li, dressed in his usual dark business suit, that is neither out of, nor in fashion, offered his shy, self-effacing smile to each guest. Victor, who seems bent on imitating his dad at every turn, was dressed almost identi-cally. But, unlike his father, Victor does not emanate a rich, complicated personality; instead, he stares too hard into his questioner's eyes and rarely if ever smiles. But then, with the weight and responsibility of being his father's point man in Canada growing daily, he likely finds little to laugh about.

Throughout the party that followed Li's introduction, dozens of business cards were pressed on Li, and a provincial representative virtually bowed and heaped praise on the tycoon for bestowing some kind of mysterious corporate blessing on Alberta. It may actually have worked, because the boys at Alberta's provincial office in Hong Kong would later acknowledge that Li's decision to buy into the province unleashed a flood of enquiries. Still, to date, Li has been the only major Hong Kong figure to invest in Alberta.

Standing not far away from Li on that warm May day in the Husky skyscraper were his two formidable captains in his assault on corporate Canada: the suave Magnus and the tough-as-nails Murray. Murray, looking, as always, tanned and fit, was at his amicable best. While his boss tried to engage his hosts in his clipped English conversation, Murray was never far away; he was always ready to rescue his boss in case things became awkward. Magnus's main job at the Husky reception seemed to be to shepherd Victor in and out of the spotlight. He thought nothing of interrupting Victor, to literally pull him away from executives and reporters who were on the verge of overwhelming the younger Li with too many questions. Just a little over a year later, there was Magnus again in Vancouver, explaining how wonderful Li Ka-shing's latest project would be for Vancouver, as Victor took his first fledgling steps from under his father's wing to head a major project in Canada.

If Li Ka-shing was later to be upset by Vancouver's reaction to the development of the Expo lands, he could take solace in the fact that he had purchased one of the prime pieces of Canadian real estate, at a bargain-basement price, on terms that would stretch over a decade. Li Ka-shing has always been lucky, but in this case, "luck" may be an inadequate word to describe his coup. After all, in this case officials from the province of British

Columbia managed to make it past the always vigilant Ezra Kwok and up the staircase to Li's office where they virtually begged the tycoon to take the property — a whopping one third of downtown Vancouver. Like the Hutchinson deal in 1977, this one was a bargain that Li could not refuse. He does not even have to pay out the entire cost of the project for fifteen years! And he only had to put $50 million down! By the time fifteen years have elapsed, the value of the property will have increased tenfold.

Despite the incredibly easy terms (the City of Vancouver or Province of British Columbia even have to pay to clean up toxic chemicals that may be present on the site), Li still played it true to form and made sure that any risk in the Expo deal was shared among some of Hong Kong's wealthiest citizens. He may have felt the need to do so, because some people involved in Hong Kong's booming property scene think that the tycoon may have slipped in Vancouver. They do not believe the city is big enough, or has the potential to grow fast enough, to accommo-date Li's ambitious plans of tacking a whole new downtown onto Vancouver.

"Spectacular" is hardly strong enough to describe what Li has in store for Vancouver. The total cost of building Pacific Place on the old Expo site could reach $2 billion. It is Li's largest investment in Canada and North America, eclipsing the almost $400 million that he paid for control of Husky. Development of the site, generally considered to be the best urban development property in North America, will be carried out by Concord Pacific Development, which will operate as a private company headed by Victor. Although opposition to the deal would later explode over charges that bidding for the property was con-ducted unfairly, and that the project was ill-suited to Vancou-ver, Li clearly won because he had the highest bid and the best project: a futuristic combination of housing, commercial tow-ers, a hotel, and even a high-tech international financial centre that will allow Vancouver to exploit its unique geographic location, while reinforcing its claim that it is truly North America's gateway to Asia. Said Magnus while detailing the plans for new financial centre: "Vancouver can deal with money markets of the world around the clock. . . . That is a tremendous advantage that no other city except Los Angeles and San Francisco has."

Many property analysts believe that Li will win his gamble in Vancouver, simply because prime land is so scarce in the west-coast city. To help make sure that he does not fail, Li brought in extra help. Although the exact figures were never released, it is believed that Li will keep over 50 per cent of the deal and will share the remaining costs with Henderson Land founder and chairman, Lee Shau-kee, and New World Holdings chairman, Cheng Yu-tung. Both men are almost the same age as Li, and share a similar background. Like Li, Lee Shau-kee came to Hong Kong in the early 1940s and was a property developer almost from the outset. While Lee Shau-kee holding's are far less in Canada than Li's, he has shown signs of wanting more. Last year, on a tour of the Toronto area, he purchased a share in a large swath of a $600-million residential housing project. Like Li, he enjoys golf and is a philanthropist, sending outstanding Hong Kong students to further their studies at Oxford. Cheng Yu-tung arrived in the Portuguese territory of Macau, located near Hong Kong at the mouth of the Pearl River, at the age of fifteen, and later made his fortune in property and jewelry. Cheng, who last year bought his first hotel in Vancouver while also buying heavily into the highly expansionist International Semi-Tech of Markham, is something of a fatalist. He likes to counsel that one should make good use of opportunity and believes that the secret to success lies in those old Calvinist principles of hard work and diligence. He likely practises his own philosophy because, in net terms, he is considered to be the second-richest man in Hong Kong.

If successful, Li's spectacular project could go a long way toward making Vancouver a booming financial centre for Asian business. But Vancouver, the nation's third-largest city, came close to losing Li, and literally billions of dollars' worth of Asian investment, when rumors surfaced that the fix was in, that someone close to the provincial government had been awarded the Expo property. Li, who desperately wants to cultivate an image that he is above reproach in Canada, came close to backing out when he felt his integrity was being questioned. It is widely believed that only a personal appeal by Vander Zalm kept him in the project. But if Li could have foreseen the problems that lay ahead, he just may have dropped out. The consequences of such a pullout would have been stunning in their enormity for B.C.

Indeed, Vancouver residents, who are only now recovering from the 1981-82 recession, the worst since the Great Depression, probably have no idea how lucky they are that Li stayed with the project. They need only to ask Jean-Pierre Guay and his fellow investment counselors at the Government of Quebec offices in Hong Kong about how the colony's investors hate political turmoil. In December, 1988, when the Government of Quebec's angry reaction to a Supreme Court ruling against some elements of Quebec's contentious language law was reported in the colony's main daily newspaper, *The South China Morning Post*, Quebec officials in the colony were horrified. The Chinese, who are extremely sensitive to the swings in political temper, will avoid Quebec if the province is seen to be tilting toward a racial battle over language. Similarly, if Li had been shut out of Vancouver by dubious politics, or baseless charges that the Chinese were somehow taking over the city, investment from Hong Kong in the city would have slowed dramatically.

Just weeks after signing the Expo deal, Vander Zalm was accused of jeopardizing the delicate balance of image and reality that now weighs in favor of Hong Kong investment in the province. The problem started innocently enough when Victor engineered the sale of a 216-unit condominium complex by a company in which he is a limited partner. But when word flashed through Vancouver's investment circles that the complex had been sold only to Hong Kong buyers, an argument over the future of the nearby Expo 86 site exploded, blasting away the thin veneer of racial harmony in Vancouver. The lowbrow Vancouver tabloid, *The Province*, not only reflected but added to the growing intolerance over the exclusive condo sale with the screaming headline: "Restricted To Buddies."

And even as Victor Li carved traces in the snow high above Vancouver at the Whistler ski resort, Vander Zalm, as if propelled by his own sense of the growing anxiety over Asian immigration to the city, sent a terrible, if not ridiculous message back to Hong Kong, by suggesting that he wanted to reopen the then eight-month-old, $320-million Expo lands sale in order to gain assurances that the property will not be resold for a quick profit, and that planned housing units would not again be sold only to offshore buyers. The premier's logic was badly twisted: after selling the site on incredibly easy terms to Li, who is Hong Kong's most celebrated citizen and clearly a foreigner, the premier then wanted assurances from Li that he would not sell it again exclusively to non-Canadians, and to top it all off, he now wanted to reopen the deal.

If there was one bright spot in the ensuing fiasco, it was that the controversy gave Victor his first chance to fly solo — and he piloted skillfully around the problem. And the always immaculate Magnus was nowhere in sight. When he came down from Whistler, Victor's first move was to admit that he had misjudged the mood of the increasingly worried city: "I was not sensitive enough to local feelings and I misjudged the market response and the immense demand for the project." Victor then traveled to Vander Zalm's aptly named theme park, "Fantasy Garden." There, much to the relief of the Vancouver politicians and businessmen, the premier backed down. Hong Kong investors would be reassured to learn that that old canon of British law, the contract, still mattered in Vancouver. "A deal is a deal," said the premier to the younger Li. Victor said that in their racist rage people forgot that he was a Canadian, and not a Chinese citizen. With an astute grasp of the situation before him, Victor referred obliquely to a problem that Canadians will have to deal with more as the amount of Hong Kong money flowing into Canada increases, that he may have been a victim of discrimination: "If I was just your average developer, thinking just of dollars and cents, then my answer would be yes. But I am not your average developer. I made my biggest investment about six years ago when I became a Canadian and British Columbian. I came 10,000 miles to make friends, not enemies, not controversies."

Where Li and his family head for from here is anyone's guess. But clearly their strategy increasingly involves Canada. Li says that he will continue to invest in the staples of life: shelter, food and energy. He says that because Canada contains an abundance of some of those commodities, he will likely invest more here. Once North American stock markets stabilize, he may raise cash for more acquisitions directly in Canada by listing his family's prime company Cheung Kong on the Toronto Stock Exchange. Says Li: "Canada is a young country. I think it has tremendous potential for growth." Such a move would make sense if Li is going to continue to purchase Canadian assets, which Canadian investors would likely buy into. One thing is certain, however, and that is that Li gets a thrill out of making money: "I enjoy business so I continue to work." And there is no reason to believe that Li, who over the past thirty-five years has raised the business of making money to an art, won't increasingly invest in Canada. A casual glance at Li's plain quartz watch provides further evidence of this. It is set to run exactly eight minutes fast. Among the highly superstitious Chinese, eight is also a symbol for good luck and making money, so there is no reason to believe that Li's troubles in Vancouver will slow his assault on corporate Canada.

3/ HO AND THE THREE MUSKETEERS

Stanley Ho, tall, elegant, sporting unfashionably long sideburns, spins a nifty fox-trot. The trim, multibillionaire casino magnate, who keeps one wife in a drafty mansion in Toronto, and another in the steamy gambling mecca of Macau, while he works alone in his black skyscraper in Hong Kong, likes to dance so much that he once matched technique with the British female ballroom dance champion. With his back and neck elegantly arched, gracefully gliding in four-four time, he cast an image utterly uncharacteristic of his fellow Hong Kong billionaires: a carefree, freewheeling, even decadent tycoon, who enjoys spending his money as much as making it. Ho represents a rare, and from the Western point of view, refreshing departure from the dreary work-until-you-drop attitude of most the colony's driven moneymen.

Round-faced, thick-nosed, big-eared Cheng Yu-tung likes gold and diamonds and, lately, Canadian property — lots and lots of Canadian property, from a vast tract of residential land near

Toronto that, when developed, will be worth almost $1 billion, to a piece of Li Ka-shing's Expo land. And, if Cheng can find one of Canada's wealthiest families or a company that would be willing to part with it, he says that he would also like to buy one of those great Canadian cash-cows, the trust company. Unlike Ho, Cheng, who is generally considered to be Hong Kong's fourth-richest citizen, is not the most flamboyant of operators. But, like Li Ka-Shing, Cheng is also a native of the Chinese province of Guangdong, and like Li, Cheng loves to play golf. And if you are a billionaire duffer who wants to be loved by Beijing's bosses when they arrive in 1997, you naturally have the legendary Arnold Palmer design your own golf course, and you build it just a long-drive and a short-putt away from the Chinese border at Chung Shan Hot Springs. "I like golf, especially when the weather is cool," said Cheng. "I used to swim a lot. But my doctor said the water in my private pool is too cold for swimming in winter. So I play golf instead."

Lee Shau-kee is known around Hong Kong as the colony's Third Musketeer, the first being property baron Li Ka-shing, and the second, jewelry, gold and real estate czar Cheng Yu-tung. Like his two close friends, Lee has just turned sixty years of age, and like them, came to Hong Kong in the 1940s and almost immediately invested in cheap land. Later, in the 1960s, he would make a spectacular fortune when Hong Kong property prices exploded. Lee, whose affected smile often dissolves into a disconcerting, shark-like grin, heads a vast corporate empire. Like Li and Cheng, he loves real estate, and like theirs, his taste is increasingly for Canadian property. Last year, Lee also took a piece of Li's Expo land to help his fellow Musketeer hedge his risk on the spectacular Vancouver project. More recently, he rolled through Toronto on a property-buying junket. With him in the Cadillac cruising down the 401 highway was William Doo, Cheng Yu-tung's millionaire partner. As they slowed down to check one tract of prime real estate near Brampton,

Lee, with a seasoned eye for a lucrative property deal, quickly spotted a fortune, and now, along with Cheng, he will build a housing development worth nearly $1 billion on the site. And he is looking for more, lots more.

The corporate empires controlled by these three powerful billionaires, Stanley Ho, Cheng Yu-tung and Lee Skau-kee, rank just below Li Ka-shing's in expanse, and all four share a growing interest in Canada, a common past and a huge two-headed problem. Li, Cheng and Lee, all fled China at different times, and along with Ho, all have good reason to doubt that their futures will continue to be so plush, wealthy and secure under the communist Chinese. Ho has been particularly straightforward on this score: At one point, he committed the grave sin of openly doubting the wisdom of continuing to invest in Hong Kong, and predicted that capital would soon flood out of the colony. But more than politics may be behind his pessimism. His family, one of Hong Kong's oldest, lost a fortune in the 1930s. His father fled the colony in disgrace and his mother was forced to pawn her jewelry to keep what remained of the family in Hong Kong alive. Now Ho, who worked so hard to restore his family's honor by rebuilding its empire, somewhat predictably warns that fortunes can just as easily vanish again if his fellow Musketeers and China fumble the homecoming of the wealthy and booming colony. Like Li Ka-shing, Stanley Ho, Cheng Yu-tung and Lee Shau-kee are all trying desperately to make sure that their families and empires continue to grow after 1997. Their elaborate strategy involves a carefully thought-out balancing act. They must keep Beijing happy by continuing to invest in the colony and in China, while protecting their own fortunes by sending money, and far more importantly from Canada's point of view, family abroad.

Next to Li's strategy of actually sending his sons here to oil the transfer of some of their assets, only Stanley Ho has crafted a bigger presence in Canada. He has done it by moving family to

Toronto, buying two of Vancouver's top hotels and investing in the Canadian fashion sector. But by far his most spectacular coup was to successfully swing a three-way deal involving elite Hong Kong investors like Cheng Yu-tung, Beijing's top economic planners, and International Semi-Tech Microelectronics Inc., a small but incredibly ambitious suburban Toronto computer manufacturer. As a result, Ho has placated China with jobs, investment, foreign markets and high-tech know-how, while allowing Hong Kong investors to get some of their cash out of the colony by investing in Semi-Tech. But more importantly for the troubled Ho, he can move some of his assets out of the colony, while at the same time showing Beijing that it is to her advantage to leave the fox-trotting tycoon's empire intact after 1997.

Canada is indeed witnessing a transfer of Hong Kong royalty to her shores as Beijing's fist rapidly closes, and the Ho family are the bluest of the colony's blue bloods to arrive. Increasingly, members of this Asian clan are making their presence felt in Toronto where they are renovating their Bridle Path mansion, attending private schools and public universities, opening top-notch restaurants and working with their latest, and highflying project, Semi-Tech. In fact, if Burke's Peerage were to open a shop in Hong Kong, references to the famous, and at one time tragic Ho family, would fill page after page. Recalls Ho: "I belong to one of the very wealthiest and oldest Hong Kong families. But when my father went bankrupt it changed my entire life. I got to know the meaning of real poverty and what it meant to lose face in Chinese society in the harshest possible way." But a walk past the black iron gates guarding the entrance of their spectacular Toronto home reveals just how high the Hos have soared since the collapse of their fabulous fortune in the 1930s.

The Ho family history reads like the turbulent, colorful and often violent history of the colony itself. His grandfather was Ho Fook, a famous overseer of Jardine, one of the largest and most famous of the colony's hongs, and his granduncle was Sir

Robert Hotung. His uncles Ho Sai-wing, Ho Saiu-yiu and Ho Leung were compradors, respectively, of the Hong Kong and Shanghai Bank, the Mercantile Bank and Jardine. His own father, Ho Kwong, was comprador to the colony's legendary Assoon family. Stanley Ho's mother, known across southeast Asia for her great beauty, was the daughter of Sin Tak-fun, a distinguished member of Hong Kong's legal fraternity and one-time chairman of the prestigious Chinese Club.

But disgrace exacts a heavy price from the highest levels of Hong Kong society: in the 1930s a failed, but entirely brave gamble on the Jardine Matheson shares ripped the Ho family asunder. Recalls Ho: "The trouble was that they all believed that because of family involvement [in Jardine] they knew everything that there was to know, but as it turned out, heavy speculation in Jardine shares spelt disaster for us all." Sir Robert Hotung, who emerged miraculously unscathed from the Jardine debacle, rescued his adoptive son Ho Sai-wing, but Ho Sai-yiu and Ho Leung tried to restore honor to their name by committing suicide and Stanley Ho's father fled to the former South Vietnamese capital of Saigon. The sense of shame that hung over the family was so palpable that one branch of the family actually took on the name Hotung, to establish a distinction between the fallen and the survivors.

Memories of that troubled time are still vivid for Ho. He says that he can clearly recall the day when he joined his family on their long journey from their luxurious home on Hong Kong's prestigious MacDonnell Road to a modest borrowed house on the much more pedestrian Caine Road. The family's summer resort, Stanley Lodge, after which he was named, was auctioned off. It was not until 1983 that Ho finally, and symbolically, managed to reacquire the oceanfront property with its spectacular beach. Recalls Ho: "My father took all my brothers with him, because they were wage-earners, and left me with my mother and sisters. He did not come back until long after I had built up my success with Macau."

And like the sudden death of Li Ka-shing's father, the shattering collapse of the Ho family fortune required young Stanley Ho to make some sudden, crucial decisions in his life. When he was thirteen, his mother, Flora, confronted him with an ultimatum: if he could not get a scholarship to continue studying at Hong Kong's prestigious Queen's College, then the family could no longer support him, and he would have to go out and work. It was a frightening option: ". . . until that time, I had been an apathetic student, but the impetus was exactly what I needed. I achieved the record of being the first D-stream student to become a scholar."

The scholarship saved Ho from menial labor in one of Hong Kong's stinking back-street factories, but just barely: "The weekends when other students' families would visit were awful. My mother simply could not afford to come, so I just stayed on there with the Jesuit fathers. That is why, I suppose, that I consistently led the field in science for the two years I was there — I had nothing else to do. I was so poor that I couldn't even afford to buy tennis balls, so as you can imagine, any sort of sport was out of the question." Although Ho's fortune, built in the gambling dens of Macau, has little to do with his background as a science major, he finds little, if anything, surprising about that: "Rich men's sons are rarely scholastically brilliant — my own children certainly did not make the grade for Hong Kong university. I am sure that if it had not been for the challenge and awfulness of our situation then, I would not be half as successful as I am now." Ho's early troubles appear to have made him compassionate and offer a clear insight into why the casino magnate is relocating some of his family members to Canada: "I, of course, maintain my commitments to my family. Even those who never helped me in the bad times are on my payroll now."

Of all the powerful Hong Kong magnates who are moving money to Canada, this ancient Hong Kong family is by far the most interesting and colorful. To reach the centre of Ho's empire, travelers must descend the steps beneath Ho's twin-towered Shun Tak Centre which lead to the colony's main ferry terminal. Of course, Ho just happens to own that as well. In the terminal they join thousands of tourists and business com-muters. While Ho works relentlessly above them on the thirty-sixth floor, most of the seaborne commuters are heading to their homes on other parts of Hong Kong Island, and many others (about five and a half million a year) take a forty-five minute ride in one of the many hydrofoils that seem to constantly be shoot-ing out from under Ho's towering office to Macau, the ancient Portuguese settlement at the mouth of China's Pearl River.

It is in Macau that Ho spins much of the money that is now finding its way to Canada. Macau, like Hong Kong, was founded by murderous pirates, romantic explorers, resolute traders and soldiers who wanted to build a trading route up the slow-moving Pearl River to Canton. The Portuguese established their settlement at the mouth of the Pearl in 1557, but their presence was not officially scknowledged by the Chinese until 1563, when Lisbon wisely sent a fleet of heavily armed warships up the Pearl to rescue a group of Chinese provincial officials who were locked in a bloody battle with roving gangs of thieves and pirates. The apparently eternally grateful Chinese author-ities gave their brave rescuers the right to occupy Macau indefi-nitely at a yearly rate of 500 gold taels. The Portuguese, who mistakenly thought that they had finally opened China up to foreign trade, later annexed their tiny piece of the Asian giant in 1887.

Macau grew in the shadow of Hong Kong — it never came close to reaching the importance of its mighty neighbor. And, unlike Hong Kong's sophisticated population, which believes that it can institute some form of democratic constitution before the Chinese arrive in 1997, Macau's modern residents have always conducted their affairs under a give-and-take arrange-ment with China: Macau could undertake its own urban and political affairs, but only with the approval of China. In short, Macau never amounted to more than a tiny, powerless Chinese territory that was operated under the Portuguese flag, but only as long as China agreed to let it.

While Li Ka-shing, Cheng Yu-tung and Lee Ka-shee fled to Hong Kong to escape the Japanese, Ho escaped to Macau just before the Japanese Emperor's army overran the colony. In hindsight it was a fortunate move, because it was in that rotting, sub-tropical backwater that Ho would find the fortune that would restore his family honor. In Macau, Ho went to work for a Japanese trading company peddling gold, toys and textiles. Having learned his craft, he opened a company of his own. Recalls Ho: "During the war years, there were lots of opportunities. You made your million very easily." His big break came in 1962, when he won the public tender for Macau's gambling monopoly. In just a few years he would restore his family to the pinnacle of wealth and respect in Hong Kong from which they had so tragically fallen some thirty years earlier.

Today, Ho owns practically everything worth having in Macau. He celebrates his glamorous holdings every year by welcoming in the Lunar New Year gambling season with the Macau governor. Ho, immaculately dressed and aristocratic in bearing, usually arrives at the old, run-down and somewhat tacky Lisboa Hotel — one of five he owns — in a Rolls-Royce. Although Ho rarely gambles, at least openly, the two men traditionally lay the first bets in a game which may earn the casino magnate as much as $400 million annually. Ho's empire in Macau also includes a greyhound racetrack, the jai alai stadium and a major slice of the corporation providing electricity to the colony, Macau Electric EGM. About 8 per cent of Macau's population depends for work on Ho's holding company, Sociedade de Turismo e Diversoes de Macau. Ho's enterprise will draw about five and a half million gamblers annually and royalties that Sociedade pays for the gambling contracts accounts for 45 per cent of the Macau government budget.

But with gambling come risks. In the summer of 1987, Ho's private secretary, Thomas Chung, was hacked to death in front of a large number of women and children outside a tennis court where the two men regularly played. The police said that the killer used a heavy-bladed knife and that the attack was meant to leave Chung paralysed for life. The murderer, as is often the case in sometimes-violent Hong Kong, was never caught, but police said that attack may have been a "payback" or warning from gangsters who, two weeks earlier, were reportedly trying to "muscle in" on the fringes of Ho's empire. Ho attended the funeral of his old friend, despite the implicit threat. Walking with a slight limp, he approached the coffin and, for a long moment, let his white-gloved hand rest on the wood and metal lid. Incredibly, although police later said the incidents were not related, just a few weeks later a second wealthy businessman was gunned down at virtually the same site where Cheng was murdered. This was not Ho's first brush with Hong Kong's aggressive underworld. In the spring of 1986, a packed Hong Kong High Court courtroom was told that a criminal gang planned to kidnap the billionaire, but the attempt was botched and ended in a wild shootout with police.

Of the four multibillionaires, Ho, Li, Lee and Cheng, Ho has the most to lose when the Chinese formally take over Hong Kong and Macau. That is probably why he is moving so much cash into Canada. While the Chinese government might find it difficult to take over Li Ka-shing's flagship, Cheung Kong (Holdings) Ltd., which is widely held on the Hong Kong Stock Exchange, they might find it morally correct to take over Ho's gambling empire, which is controlled by only a few men, including Ho's close personal friend Cheng Yu-tung. Gambling, after all, is illegal in China. This was what Ho believed in 1984, shortly after Hong Kong and Britain concluded the agreement to return the colony to China. Ho predicted at that time that vast amounts of cash would flow out of the two colonies, and that more would find its way to safe havens before the transfer. He obviously had very little faith in Beijing's ability to balance capitalism — particularly the brash style practised in Hong Kong — and the doctrinaire Marxism that was then in fashion in China.

Initially, Ho's misgivings about China's future handling of the colony and its small club of multibillionaires led him to float the idea of taking his casino operation public. Hong Kong investors, who follow Ho and The Three Musketeers into almost any venture, were rumored ready to buy a piece of the gambling empire. By going public, Ho believed that even though gambling was illegal in Hong Kong and China, the colony's post-1997 masters would find it difficult to nationalize his company, particularly if parts of the investment were held by off-shore owners. But Ho's initial pessimism was tempered some-what in 1987 when China agreed to take Macau back in 1999, but at the same time promised, although Ho's gambling empire was not specifically mentioned, that the colony's economic system would remain untouched until 2049. For whatever rea-son, but probably to prevent a loosening of his corporate domi-nance, Ho finally ended months of speculation in 1988 and called off the share issue, saying, "we really do not need the money." Or, his decision to not go public may have been bravado. Ho, despite his position in the colony, simply may not have been able to find investors willing to back his casino issue because there was no guarantee that China would not crush his operation in 1999, or at least take a healthy piece of Ho's gambling profits.

Ho now says that he does trust the Chinese to leave his gambling empire alone after 1997 and 1999, but he is still build-ing an elaborate plan to hold the Chinese at bay by turning his firm into a critical, and he hopes, indispensable, cog in China's drive to modernize its industries. In 1988 that strategy would be suddenly indicated by two bold corporate moves: Ho would locate part of his family in Canada and buy into International Semi-Tech Microelectronics Inc. By moving some family mem-bers to Canada, he would be able to shelter part of his fortune in North America, while Semi-Tech would provide an appeasing conduit of cash into and out of China. So far his ambitious play for Semi-Tech is working and Hong Kong investors are lining up to back it.

Indeed, of all the strategies hatched by Hong Kong's rich and powerful elite to hold China off in 1997, Ho's Semi-Tech play is clearly the most interesting. Until 1987 Semi-Tech was a tiny designer and manufacturer of personal computers whose revenues had never exceeded $27 million in a single year. By 1989 it was battling to complete its fourth major acquisition in the incredibly short span of just eleven months. And yet, few investment analysts in Canada seemed to be aware that it was Ho who was fueling this incredible expansion drive. Semi-Tech's most ambitious move was a $300-million buyout of Shelton, Connecticut–based Singer Sewing Machine Co. (SSMC). With the Singer purchase the suburban Toronto firm has grown from just another small computer manufacturer to a worldwide conglomerate with $1.8 billion in annual revenues. Says Semi-Tech president James Ting: "When Ho invests in something, things happen." For Ting, the most important element of Ho's involvement is his ability to bring other investors in.

Semi-Tech was created in 1981 by the hard-driving Ting, a Shanghai-born, Canadian-educated engineer and workaholic bachelor, who says that he does not have time to even consider a family, in his attempt to build what he describes as an "Eastern-style business in the West." Like many Chinese immigrants, he dreams big dreams. He wants to build an empire to rival huge Asian conglomerates such as Japan's Mitsubishi Corp., in which manufacturing, resource, trading, banking and insurance companies support one another's activities under one corporate roof. Ting just may succeed: he has already struck an unprecedented accord with China, where Semi-Tech is now developing consumer products that will be sold by Semi-Tech's eighty-seven Consumers Distributing Co. Ltd. outlets in the eastern United States. Consumers is the third largest catalogue-showroom company in that country.

It would be a gross understatement to suggest that Ting's biggest break came when "one of our documents came to Ho's attention." Ho immediately recognized the possibilities inherent in the unique manufacturing agreement with China. It was one that he would exploit in a big way. Ting had negotiated the agreement with the government of the Chinese province of Shenzhen in October, 1986. It entered Semi-Tech and the Shenzhen Electronics Group (SEG) into a $270-million research and development deal. The plan, which will eventually allow SEG to manufacture microcomputers in Shenzhen, is the largest ever signed between a Canadian private–sector company and a Chinese firm. SEG, in turn, took the unusual step of purchasing a 5.9 per cent interest in Semi-Tech's Asian manufacturing branch, Semi-Tech Microelectronics (Far East) Ltd.

Ting met with Ho on a number of occasions leading up to Semi-Tech's listing on the Hong Kong Stock Exchange. With the powerful and influential Ho now behind the firm, its shares virtually sold out. The company was able to raise $55 million by selling 49 per cent of its stock to Hong Kong investors. To lead the way and create confidence, Ho and his old friend Cheng Yu-tung, each bought $8.1 million worth of stock. Shortly after the listing, Ting invited Ho to become chairman of Semi-Tech (Far East). If any Hong Kong investors had been reluctant to invest in Semi-Tech before then, the presence of Ho as chairman blasted away any doubts that may have remained. Says Ting: "We have a very close relationship. He is putting his reputation on the line and saying, 'I'm betting on James Ting.' He wants to get more involved."

Within days of signing on with Ting, Ho was in action, flying Semi-Tech officials down to New Jersey in his Lear jet to inspect the Consumers outlets. While the Consumers deal seems out-of-step for a computer firm, it fits perfectly into Ting's and Ho's plan to use China's cheap labor to manufacture products to sell through the chain. And that strategy crystalized when Semi-Tech announced that it had concluded yet another joint-venture agreement with SEG for the design and development of consumer electronic products, including VCRs and TV sets for the Consumers chain. The Chinese will manufacture the appliances and private–label brands for Consumers and other companies, such as Sears Roebuck & Co. Ultimately these items could be sold under the SSMC label. That is why the acquisition of SSMC was critical for Ho's and Ting's plan. They will now be able to source and manufacture computer and consumer products on a very economical basis in the Far East and plug those products into SSMC's 100-country distribution network.

While Semi-Tech, propelled by Ho's now rising interest in the firm, was building inroads into China and North America, Ho was also touring the shop floor of a prominent Canadian data processing operation. He obviously liked what he saw and in March 1988, just three weeks after the announcement of the Consumers purchase, Semi-Tech bought DataCrown Corp., the computer services division of Crowntech Inc., for an un-disclosed sum. Then, in June, Semi-Tech acquired Canada Systems Group Ltd., Canada's leading supplier of data process-ing services, for $56.6 million. Through the two takeovers, Semi-Tech captured more than 700 clients, including T. Eaton Co., Stelco Inc. and the federal government, as well as many small companies. Ho's broad plan seemed to be taking shape: Semi-Tech now had a built-in market for their own computer products.

Ho's decision to exploit Ting's link to China points to one of the critical benefits that Hong Kong money will play in the years leading up to 1997. As well, it is a shining example of how Canadian businessmen can tap the flood of money leaving Hong Kong. At the end of 1988, Ting had only been able to raise a paltry $5.1 million on Toronto's timid Bay Street, through his initial public offering in December, 1986. While Toronto's investment community constantly criticized Ting for growing too fast, investors in New York and Hong Kong recognized the awesome potential in his China connection and his powerful backer, Ho. They were only too happy to invest when given the opportunity. As Li Ka-shing's presence at his Calgary reception underscored, Hong Kong investment may become the single most important area of new financing to wash over Canada in years. Clearly, if the Canadian investment community won't back a small firm — or large ones for that matter — Hong Kong tycoons like Ho, Cheng Yu-tung and Li Ka-shing will.

In addition to their development of Semi-Tech, members of the Ho family have been busy elsewhere in Canada, particularly in Vancouver where they recently bought two of that city's newest downtown hotels. In September, 1988, Ho bought Vancouver's Le Meridien Hotel for $47.7 million, and a few days later he bought the next-door apartment hotel, La Grande Residence, for another $22 million. Both hotels were little more than one and a half years old and were built for Expo 86. Ho plays only a small role in the management of the hotels. Unlike his old friend Cheng Yu-tung, who prefers to dismiss almost the entire management when he buys an existing hotel, Ho has left the management intact. In fact, in the seventeen months after the billionaire bought it, he only stopped by once, and then just long enough to say hello. Ho has an interest in the Toronto garment industry through his wife, Lucina Laam and her sister Eliza Kuok. They have invested $450 million in KHK Fashion Group, an upscale clothing, designing and manufacturing company in the Spadina textile district. It was their fashions that were on display at a 1988 charity attended by Ho in Toronto.

As Stanley Ho's defensive strategy unfolds further as 1997 draws nearer, Canadians will be able to count the ancient Hong Kong family as one of the most interesting, controversial and important Hong Kong clans ever to splinter off into this country. And Ho was at his flamboyant best when he made his splashy entrance into Canadian corporate society at the charity ball, which was organized by his dynamic, ninety-eight-pound eldest daughter, Pansy, and KHK co-owner, Peggy Chan. The event, staged at Li Ka-shing's Harbour Castle Westin hotel in Toronto, raised $200,000 for Toronto's Hospital for Sick Children and for a nursing home for senior citizens from the city's Chinese community. While Li Ka-shing had worn his customary dark business suit, and bowed and chatted politely at his coming-out party in Calgary, Ho displayed the flair of a gambling baron, wearing a black tuxedo and a silver bow tie.

While one of Hong Kong's top crooners sang in the background, Ho, tall, elegant and always charming, spent the evening warmly and comfortably greeting guests, while cameras recorded his every move. Lucina wore a black-lace Christian Dior dress, but as usual, methodically avoided the spotlight, and is hard to spot in any of the hundreds of photos and hours of videotape of the event. In his address to the blue-chip crowd, Ho said that one of the main reasons he decided to move Lucina to Toronto was for her personal safety. Said Ho: "My charming wife, Lucina, who is with me tonight, tells me how happy she is living here. I am not worried anymore about her safety, because every other person she meets in Toronto is from Hong Kong. I recognize how strong our presence is in Canada and the debt we owe to the generous people of this great country to make us so welcome here."

Ho visits Canada only about six times a year. While he flies around the world looking for new investments, Lucina lives quietly in their Bridle Path mansion with her children and her father. Pansy, her older daughter, lives in Hong Kong and works as a vice-president of public relations for Semi-Tech's Hong Kong branch. (This underlines an important point that Canadian business will have to come to terms with: when Hong Kong's rich and powerful decide to inject a substantial amount of cash into a Canadian firm, they usually send a family member along to keep an eye on their investment.) Pansy, like her father, is flamboyant and outgoing, and is known throughout the colony for her charity galas, for which invitations are always coveted because of the top entertainment she brings in. Her "Viennese Opera Ball" was the highlight of the Hong Kong society season, raising $3.2 million (HK).

The Hos have even managed to brighten The Bridle Path. Their palatial, $5.4-million brown-and-red Toronto house has a Middle Eastern flavor with a large square tower topped by narrow brick arches. The building, with two swimming pools and a giant indoor hot tub, rises behind black iron gates where the Harbridge & Cross construction company is carrying out millions of dollars' worth of renovations. In typically secretive, Hong Kong style, the work crews have been ordered to say nothing about their work. Like the presence of Li Ka-shing's family in Canada, Ho's decision to locate here is considered a major selling point for other Hong Kong residents. Even before the renovations were completed, the house became an attraction for visitors and would-be immigrants from the colony, who constantly parade past, hoping for a glimpse of the illustrious Hong Kong blue bloods. Still, while Lucina's house in Hong Kong always buzzed with the excitement generated by her constant entertaining, she is now a shadowy and withdrawn figure, preferring to remain inside her giant home where she spends her days reading, playing Chinese musical instruments or making Chinese brush paintings. Says Pansy: "My mother likes being in Canada. She is a quiet person. Her only habit is reading." Like most wealthy Hong Kong women, Lucina does like to shop, but on a level that few people ever reach. To furnish her spectacular home, Lucina took a number of buying sprees in Europe to purchase fifteenth- and sixteenth-century European antiques.

Pansy says that her father does, indeed, keep two wives, but she repeatedly makes the point that Hong Kong law recognizes multiple marriages consummated before 1972, the year that the ancient practice was outlawed. Stanley Ho still visits both wives, but only rarely: Lucina says that she expects to see her husband in Toronto about three times a year. Ho has been prolific over the years, producing three daughters from the first marriage, and five, including Pansy, from the marriage to Lucina. But despite the size of his family, Stanley Ho apparently prefers to live alone. Said Pansy: "I cannot describe it. It is all very strange."

It was Lucina herself who decided to buy a house in Toronto and immigrate to Canada. Her decision, like that made by so many other Hong Kong residents, was based in part on acquiring Canadian citizenship, a better education and the need to be near older members of the family. Lucina's father had moved to

Canada ten years earlier and other relatives are also here. According to Pansy, the family did not decide to come to Canada just for political reasons. "It was not a political reason to move to Canada. We did not have any worries about 1997," she says. "My father has a Portuguese passport, so we can escape from Hong Kong whenever we want to." Instead, she claims that the family came to Canada, as so many Chinese immigrants before them, for education. "My mother chose to move here. She finds life in Hong Kong very frantic. And she felt that my youngest sister and brother were reaching the age when they would benefit from a Canadian education." Still, to hear Pansy use the words "escape from Hong Kong" reveals much about the underlying drive behind their decision to abandon their tropical home and a life-style they clearly love for a home on Toronto's staid Bridle Path.

Pansy paints a complicated portrait of her father. On the one hand he is a sophisticated businessman, possessing great foresight, and capable of moving easily in a modern Western setting. On the other hand, he remains closely wedded to traditional Oriental beliefs. Says Pansy: "He is a very determined person. He has a lot of confidence in himself and a lot of drive. But you could say that he is innovative in business but traditional in his attitudes toward women. He does not believe in women working. He does not tell me that he disapproves of me working, but he does not take what I do very seriously. He prefers it when I do charity work." Like most anyone capable of carving a multi-billion-dollar empire in the intense Hong Kong environment, Ho is a workaholic. Says Pansy: "His faults are that he is quick-tempered and impatient. He makes it hard for other people to keep up, at work or at home. He does not know how to relax as other people do."

While Ho and Li Ka-shing have built high-profile defensive strategies involving Canada in preparation for 1997, their close friend Cheng Yu-tung has taken note, and is now not far behind. Canadian businessmen hunting for a joint-venture partner should also take note. He may soon overtake the wealthy pair by launching a corporate initiative that has so far been ignored by Hong Kong's rich and powerful elite: he wants to buy into Canada's booming financial sector by purchasing a Canadian trust company. Sitting in the front living room of a so-called superhome, just off of Highway 401 in the upscale Toronto suburb of North York, his Canadian–educated partner, William Doo, has just returned from a scouting mission. His assignment: to locate and buy the trust company and pick up more property — lots more property — for the family, including a prime hotel site in downtown Toronto.

Back in Hong Kong, the quiet, methodical Cheng sits at the head of his flagship firm, New World Developments, and waits patiently for his scouting party to report. Apart from his love of golf, and his reputation for laying $1,000-a-hole-bets, Cheng cuts a profile in the colony that is different from those of Li, the globe-trotting *taipan*, and Ho, the flamboyant aristocrat. But all three remain constantly in the public eye for different reasons: Li, because he acquired the ancient trading hong, Hutchinson, and now his every move is analysed and weighed for insight into what he plans to do in 1997; Ho, because of his family's ancient eminence in the colony, and his penchant for high-profile, controversial ventures; and Cheng, because, while he rarely boasts or seeks the media's attention in the colony, his New World nameplate proudly hangs on some of the colony's most spectacular projects. Currently, the most important of Cheng's developments is the $2 billion (HK) Hong Kong Convention and Exhibition Centre, a long, swaybacked building on the harborfront in Wan Chai.

A native of Shunduo in the province of Guangdong, Cheng was born on August 27, 1925, and fled to Hong Kong in the early 1940s. Like his fellow Musketeers, Cheng made his fortune in the 1960s and 1970s when the Hong Kong real estate market exploded in value. He incorporated New World in 1970, and by the end of 1986, had put together a land bank containing some thirty sites with the potential to encompass 11.3 million square feet of space. He is also involved in one of the most glamorous professions in money-drenched Hong Kong — jewelry and gold — through Chow Tai Fook Enterprises, the largest importer and exporter of diamonds in the colony.

So far, Cheng's highest-profile play in Canada occurred in 1988, when he teamed up with the third Musketeer, Lee Shau-kee, to help spread the risk on Li's Expo lands deal. But behind that widely publicized move (which surprised no one in Hong Kong, where the trio regularly teams up on large projects) Cheng is quietly, but rapidly expanding his empire in Canada. Again, like his high-rolling colleagues, he is moving both family and cash to Canada. Echoing Li's sentiment that "an education is the most important" of all life's endeavors, he sent his son to be educated at the University of Toronto. Ever since then, he has been a patron of the school, pumping thousands of dollars into it, and receiving an honorary doctorate in return, thanks to which he is now known as "Doctor" Cheng in Hong Kong.

Toronto first drew the Cheng family's corporate attention just a year after the British decided to return the colony to the Chinese. In 1985, the Chengs bought a large property on the southwest corner of University Avenue and Dundas Street for $10 million. The intersection, one of the busiest in the city's downtown core, will house a nineteen-story commercial tower. But Cheng's partner, William Doo, says that the building will be more than a towering slab of polished blue granite. The building is to be New World's premier development in Canada, a sky-scraping symbol that the family is here to stay. They want it to be a spectacular piece of architecture that will add to the city's skyline for decades to come. Equally important, the building sits on the northeastern edge of Toronto's downtown Chinese community where it will be a symbol of the community's new and growing strength in Canada. Indeed, the structure will pull

Chinatown symbolically toward the power-filled towers in the nation's financial heart.

Cheng's architect for the University Avenue building, the family's most important project in Canada, is Michael Wong. Wong is originally from Hong Kong, but has lived in Toronto for many years, and is a favorite of the high-rolling Musketeers: he works closely with both Li Ka-shing and Lee Shau-kee. Wong says that the Cheng family reminds him of another clan of spectacular Toronto builders: the Reichmanns. Like the Reichmanns, proprietors of an international empire controlled through Olympia & York Developments, Cheng wants to be involved in every detail of his projects, from designing floor plans to choosing materials. "He looks at every detail," says Wong. "He even remembers that the underground parking has room for 151 cars and that the building has 311,500 square feet, 18,000 square feet per floor. That is what impressed me most about Cheng. He is very knowledgeable." Cheng's Canadian-educated children, Henry and Peter, are also closely involved in the University Avenue project. Henry shares his father's penchant for detail but, perhaps because of his experience in the West, away from the colony's frantic pace, he is more light-hearted. "When you work for Henry, you will die for him," says Wong. "I can laugh with Henry. But you do not joke with Cheng Yu-tung."

Still, the Hong Kong billionaire is unfamiliar with many important aspects of business in Canada. At one point during the designing of the University Avenue building, Wong had to explain to Cheng that the ratio of costs in Hong Kong — 60 per cent for materials and 40 per cent for labor — is usually reversed in Canada, and that Cheng, unaware of how relatively well-paid Toronto's unionized construction workers are, underestimated his labor bill. Wong also tactfully coached Cheng on development etiquette in Toronto, and finally led him into meetings with the project's neighbors and surrounding community to ensure that everyone would be happy with the project. Recalls Wong: "Cheng said, 'Michael, I go to Canada to make friends. I do not want to be hit-and-run.' "

To make sure that no one walks away with that impression, Wong says that Cheng also aspires to outclass other Canadian builders. While it is too early to tell whether Cheng can, indeed, out build his fierce competitors in Toronto, he is off to a solid start with the University Avenue project. The polished, blue-granite structure will contain a towering glass atrium and the new entrance to Toronto's St. Patrick subway station. Cheng also agreed to donate a piece of the land for a social-housing project and $200,000 to the city to be used toward the construction of the project, in return for increasing its size. Cheng was likely surprised by the concessions that he had to make; he would be under no such pressure in Hong Kong where development is freewheeling and largely unregulated.

Over the next five years, the names Cheng Yu-tung and New World will no doubt become as familiar as those of Li Ka-shing and Stanley Ho in Toronto, as the family's projects — particularly their trust company play — come together. Already, the Cheng family and William Doo are constructing a 1,000-unit residential subdivision in Brampton that could be worth close to $1 billion when it is completed. And Doo is also hunting for a downtown Toronto site on which New World Developments hopes to build the first hotel in its Regent Hotel chain in Canada. Cheng tendered a bid on a piece of land just to the east of Li Ka-shing's Harbour Castle Westin, but failed to get it, even though his price may have been the top offer. That fact does not sit well with Doo who stops just short of claiming that the family was the victim of racism.

If Cheng's New World Harbourside Hotel in Vancouver, previously the Holiday Inn Harbourside, is a precedent, Cheng intends to build hotels that have an Oriental flavor. The Harbourside has been renovated to include the Dynasty Club for executives and Taipan Rooms for business functions. And given the ever-increasing number of Chinese people moving to Canada, the Cheng family's presence will only grow.

Just imagine Paul Reichmann, Conrad Black and Edgar Bronfman, or any other trio of Canadian corporate barons for that matter, teaming up to save the Toronto Stock Exchange from a dizzying collapse! But then, wide-open Hong Kong is not as highly regulated as Toronto, so the colony's reeling investment community was hardly surprised in the weeks following the October, 1987, stock market crash when Lee Shau-kee led his fellow Musketeers, Li Ka-shing and Cheng Yu-tung, to the rescue of the Hong Kong Stock Exchange's futures market. While Hong Kong governor Sir David Wilson played for time, and in true British (and certainly Canadian) fashion, called for an inquiry into the shambles on the Hong Kong Stock Exchange floor, the three multibillionaires took matters into their own hands. By pumping close to $500 million into the exchange, they slowed the collapse and slowly pushed futures contracts higher. As usual, investors followed the closely-watched three, this time back into the flattened market. The trio's wager was brave and dangerous. They invested their half billion dollars in Long Futures, meaning that they believed that the market would rise again in thirty days. If it did not, even these men would have felt the loss. As it turned out, however, they walked away $109 million wealthier, and in the process, reinforced their image as the tycoons with the Midas touch.

Not surprising then, Lee Shau-kee returned a little more than a year later with his two tycoon buddies to become the third member in a flying-wedge assault on corporate Vancouver and Toronto. British Columbia premier William Vander Zalm's sell-off of Crown-owned resources seems to particularly interest Lee, the billionaire with the shark-like grin. In June, 1988, he announced that Pacific Rim Gas, a wholly owned subsidiary of his Hong Kong and China Gas Co., would go after Mainland Gas Service, the natural gas distribution arm of the British Columbia Hydro and Power Authority. Lee, Cheng and Li had worked so closely together in previous deals that the always aggressive Hong Kong newspapers reported incorrectly that Li Ka-shing was also in on the deal. In the end, Lee failed to land Mainland Gas; if he had been successful, B.C.'s oil and gas industry may have received a major boost, because Lee planned to use his own Hong Kong and China Gas Co. to help Mainland "develop gas distribution business in other parts of the Asia Pacific Region." That is a theme that has permeated the Vander Zalm administration's rhetoric: that B.C., and particularly Vancouver, must become Canada's gateway to the Asia–Pacific market. Was Lee frozen out of the running because anti–Hong Kong sentiment was reaching fever pitch in Vancouver at the time? Perhaps. The province sent out clear signals that it preferred to keep Mainland in Canadian hands, and bound all firms bidding on Mainland to an iron-clad confidentiality agreement, to prevent any debate over the nationality of the bids in of the media.

In the months leading up to Lee's run at Mainland, he had followed Li and Cheng into the controversial development of the Expo site in Vancouver. Once again, rumors shot through Hong Kong's financial district that The Three Musketeers were in action. The high-flying trio's purchase of the Expo lands confirmed speculation in the colony that the three billionaires were solidifying into a private club, where the admission price was the ability to play a game of golf for $1 million. Says one close observer of the three: "It's a billionaires' club — who else can play golf at a million dollars a throw? Rich guys need friends, too, and rather than have guys sucking up to them, they would rather have other rich guys as friends." As in any tightly knit group of businessmen, the overriding philosophy is: I'll scratch your back if you scratch mine. Says another Hong Kong businessman: "They get to see deals that you or I will never get to see. It is very much a question of 'you let me in, I'll let you in.' They take care of each other."

That kinship was at work again in late 1988 when Lee flew to Canada to have a closer look at the booming Toronto real estate market. Lee, who had purchased a hotel in Vancouver, likes land — lots of land. And sitting with William Doo, fellow Musketeer Cheng's partner, in a Cadillac spinning out of Toronto, Lee had plenty of time to scout for buys. While some Hong Kong buyers indulge in what is known in Canadian real estate circles as the "Hong Kong starter pack" (perhaps a couple of condos, a small office building and a strip mall) Lee had his own Hong Kong starter pack in mind. He found in on the western outskirts of Toronto, in Brampton, a sprawling acreage of prime real estate. He quickly bought in. And why not? Doo was going to buy in for the Cheng family, so why not take a piece as well?

What is next for Stanley Ho, the moneyed Musketeers, Li Ka-shing, Lee Shau-kee and Cheng Yu-tung? Much of what the trio does next will depend on what they sniff in the breezes blowing in from Beijing. While their children have never known want, fear or disgrace, the four powerful tycoons can all remember harder times. If China's struggle to modernize falters under the weight of poverty, lack of resources and bureaucratic infighting, and the doctrinaire Marxists return, then the flight of capital from the colony will dramatically increase. For their part, both Ho and Cheng have argued that the colony must remain as it is for now, that any move to undertake democratic reform in the colony before 1997 would be a mistake. Indeed, Cheng believes that there could be a mass exodus from Hong Kong in the early 1990s if Hong Kong's "tried and tested" government is changed and the wrong message sent to Beijing. In fact, the colony's billionaires are so appalled at the thought of anything changing in their money factories that they are oftened blinded to the lapses in their own logic. For example, Cheng says that a one-man-one-vote system would be open to manipulation by unscrupulous politicians, who would advocate an expansion of the social welfare system.

4/ CHASING HONG KONG MONEY

The communist Bank of China's new skyscraper, the tallest in Asia, rises like a triple-edged dagger from Central, Hong Kong's financial district. For people staring skyward from the congested streets below, the arresting seventy-story, triangular tower looks like a spear, and for many, it appears to be aimed at the very heart of the colony. The building, which will soon house Beijing's central bank, casts a long, icy shadow over the nearby dome of the legislative building, and such key centres of financial power as Li Ka-shing's office and the Hong Kong & Shanghai Banking Corp. Even the *feng-shui* masters, those mysterious Chinese gentlemen who help make sure that structures are built in harmony with nature, are upset by the location and design of the building. Says Sung Siu-kwong, a forty-three-year-old *feng-shui* master: "People are afraid the sharp points will cause damage to the surroundings. It's like a knife pointing at you. It could cause bad health or economic damage."

It is the economic damage — nothing else really matters in

Hong Kong — that preoccupies the people toiling in the building's shadow. In just eight years, China will take over the colony, and the razor-edged building is a constant reminder that the clock is ticking down on their way of life. Seven out of every ten people in Hong Kong either fled from communism in China themselves, or have at least one parent who did. And, despite reassurances from Beijing, a mass exodus of people and capital is underway. Agencies that advise on emigration are prospering. Hong Kong even has its own magazine for deserters, *The Emigrant*. And the majority of people fleeing the bank's shadow are heading directly to Canada.

This stampede has Ottawa and the Canadian provinces panting. Indeed, no other Western country has engineered such a blatant grab for Hong Kong's elite and their wealth. The Australian embassy regularly rolls out the red carpet for the rich businessmen and investors who are exiting the colony daily. And, the doors of the United States embassy are always open to wealthy emigrants who want to build new businesses in the richest economy on earth. But when Hong Kong's entrepreneurs and investors really start to worry about the future, they know that the easiest haven to enter is the Commission for Canada, which is located in beautiful offices high above the harbor in a granite-sheathed tower. There, a corps of special Canadian visa officers, known as Entrepreneurial Development Officers, trained in analysing the viability of businesses and forecasting corporate cash flow, are ready to help smooth their paths into Canada.

Canada's pitchmen are also found in huge office blocks near the Bank of China where Ontario, Alberta, British Columbia, Manitoba and Quebec — even the city of Montreal — operate their own bustling trade offices, with full-time personnel specially trained to help business people set up ventures and invest within their provincial boundaries. Nearly every week, a new delegation of Canadian businessmen, government officials and

provincial premiers arrives in Hong Kong in search of investment and rich immigrants. And pin-striped Canadian lawyers
and immigration consultants, all held in contempt by federal
and provincial officials, regularly hang out their shingles. They
offer to provide to the colony's increasingly desperate businessmen with pricey, and sometimes woefully impractical, advice on how to get into Canada. Even a few Canadian investment funds, scrambling for a slice of the Hong Kong money
fleeing the colony, have opened offices there to meet with
investors on a one-on-one basis, to pre-screen applicants and,
when needed, even to help them fill out their immigration
applications.

All in all, these touts have an easy sell. Hong Kong businessmen may find the Canadian tax system oppressive, such
civilities as our minimum-wage laws excessive, and view
Toronto, Vancouver and Montreal as dull hick towns compared to their own city. But they still see Canada as a big, safe,
racially tolerant, politically stable country, with good schools for
their children. Tangible evidence of Canada's virtues abounds
in Hong Kong, where there are 80,000 Canadian-educated
people, many of whom hold top-paying, middle- and upper-
management jobs. Their confidence in Canada has been
bolstered by the likes of Li Ka-shing and others, who strategically educate and locate their offspring in Canada. Meanwhile,
publications found in waiting rooms in the city's financial district explain the Canadian system and way of life. Articles in
these magazines emphasize that, while Canadian investment and
business is still pretty staid compared to the rough-and-tumble
attitudes and practices in Hong Kong, we are getting better at
the free-enterprise game.

But the main reason Canada continues to be the favorite
destination for Hong Kong's monied elite is Ottawa's highly
publicized Business Immigration Program, which gives well-
heeled investors and business people from around the world

preferred treatment, ahead of all classes of immigrants except refugees. By far most of the activity under the program comes from Hong Kong.

Under the controversial program, business immigrants fall into three categories: self-employed business people, as well as personalities in areas such as sports or the performing arts; entrepreneurs, who have the wherewithal to start, buy and manage a business which employs at least one Canadian; and investors, who are required to sink a minimum of $250,000 in a venture — if it is in the more prosperous provinces of Ontario, Quebec, Alberta and British Columbia — for three years.

From Ottawa's point of view, the goal of the program is to bring knowledgeable business people and risk capital into Canada in an effort to boost the overall economy, to foster development in the less-developed provinces and to prevent a looming and precipitious decline in Canada's population. However, for wealthy Hong Kong residents, who regularly lay down hundreds of thousands of Hong Kong dollars for a Rolls-Royce Silver Shadow and millions for a Hollywood-style mansion on the green slopes rising from away from the city core, $250,000 is simply a cheap insurance policy against the heavy hand of communism. Says one Hong Kong banker: "People carry that much money around in their pockets." Claims Toronto condominium broker Marty Atkins who does an extensive trade with Hong Kong investors: "In Hong Kong they can turn their money three times a year. Canada — it is just a parachute."

The push to Canada began in 1984, when the residents of Hong Kong learned that the colony will revert to Chinese control at the stroke of midnight on July 1, 1997. From the time of the announcement through 1988 more than 59,951 Hong Kong immigrants arrived in Canada, including growing numbers of businessmen, professionals and managers.

In 1979, just eleven business immigrants came from Hong Kong. By 1983 the figure had soared to 338. During the period from 1984 to 1988, Hong Kong was far and away the biggest source of business immigrants to Canada, accounting for more than 4,000 of the approximately 13,000 total. These new, aggressive, highly sophisticated Hong Kong Canadians have promised to transfer an astounding $5 billion in investments and assets to Canada over the next five years, and to create or retain more than 20,000 jobs for Canadians.

But where and how? Government figures are virtually useless when it comes to following the trail of Hong Kong money and business immigrants in Canada. "No figures can reflect the whole story," says Bob Brown, Eastern region president of the HongKong Bank of Canada. "There's just too much going on. Money can come in and go out very freely. The conversion is all done somewhere else. When it gets to Canada it is already in U.S. or Canadian dollars."

Indeed, over a steaming six-course seafood lunch in an immaculate restaurant in the city's financial district, a Hong Kong billionaire told the authors that he has moved millions of dollars in bearer bonds into Canadian bank vaults. "I have even moved my collection of platinum watches to Canada," he said. But this secret flow of flight capital will never enter the calculations of even the most enterprising government auditor.

Unlike their predecessors, who primarily built traditional Chinese businesses like laundries and restaurants, these newcomers are estimated by one front man for some of the colony's billionaire citizens to be easily worth $1 million each. In many cases, they have sent to Canada as the advance guard representing a far larger fortune. And they are willing to try almost anything: a day care centre in Pickering, Ontario, a plastics plant in Weston, Ontario, a ginseng-drink import operation in Markham, Ontario, a fish-processing plant in Newfoundland, a horse-breeding farm in Campbellville, Ontario, a videotape cassette manufacturer in Thunder Bay, Ontario, and scattered garment factories, jewelry stores, hotels — lots and lots of big, expensive hotels — and acres of prime real estate.

With impressive results like that, it is not surprising that Louis Ferguson, the stocky, friendly, career civil servant who heads up Immigration Canada's business immigration department, grows frustrated whenever he is asked whether the program has been a success. Interviewed in his sparse Hull, Quebec, office in late 1988, Louis wore a dark, pin-striped, three-piece suit, and the weary attitude of someone who had answered the same tiresome question dozens of times before. "During the last generation we were looking for people to till the land. Now we are looking for people with knowledge, talent and some capital," he said in French-accented English, his voice rising: "The program is designed to address certain economic and industrial development realities. It is a success if people use it. Isn't it that simple?"

Well, hardly. Thousands of businessmen from Hong Kong and other countries may be flooding into Canada each year under the Business Immigration Program, and in the process, bolstering the economy with new money and increasing employment. But during its short history, the program has won Ottawa few political points and caused the government more than its share of headaches. Canada has certainly made enemies in the Hong Kong government, which blames Ottawa's opportunistic program for worsening the "brain drain" of entrepreneurs and skilled professionals out of the colony. And incredibly, many Hong Kong–based businesses now launch recruiting drives in Canada in a desperate attempt to lure highly educated workers and professionals back to Hong Kong, where they are badly needed.

Even the Canadian Chinese community is suspicious about Ottawa's sudden willingness to hand out visas to wealthy Asians. That is understandable. After all, Canada does not exactly have a history of generosity to Chinese immigrants. As Gary Yee, president of the Chinese Canadian National Council, puts it: "Looking at the government's early policies, it is clear that the main motivation was racism." And, Yee, in fact, may even be understating matters.

The story of the Chinese in Canada begins more than 130 years ago, with the discovery of gold in British Columbia's verdant Fraser Valley. Within weeks of the strike, hundreds of prospectors, including a number of Chinese originally from the Pearl River delta in what is now Guangdong province, left the California gold fields and converged on British Columbia. Through the newcomers, word of the Canadian strike quickly spread to China, which was then in the midst of the Taiping Rebellion, a peasant revolt that lasted from 1850 until 1864, and claimed twenty million lives. The first shipload of Chinese from Hong Kong arrived in the spring of 1859, and two years later, as many as 6,000 Chinese were thought to be toiling in the Caribou gold fields in Fraser Valley.

Many of the Chinese pioneers staked profitable claims. Others eagerly filled the gaps in the frontier economy, providing the largely male gold rush population with laundries, restaurants and vegetables grown on truck farms, building roads, stringing telegraph wires and working in the fish canneries and coal mines on Vancouver Island. It didn't take long for anti-Chinese sentiment to surface, particularly when the gold rush slowed and the local economy spiraled into a depression. By the mid-1860s, good placer mining claims had become scarce, and whites working in the gold fields increasingly viewed the Oriental newcomers as inscrutable competitors willing to undercut their wages. By the early 1870s, the gold rush had lost its glitter and the transient workers had melted away from British Columbia. That left the local government in a quandary: without increasing the population, the area could never become prosperous; at the same time, white settlers were constantly complaining about the racial origins of newcomers to the area. Efforts to exclude the "wrong kind" of settlers — which meant non-whites — gathered steam. In 1875, four years after British Columbia joined Confederation, the B.C. government passed legislation removing the Chinese from the provincial voters' list. A year later, a bill was passed prohibiting the hiring of Chinese for government projects.

Probably the main reason Canada did not shut down Chinese immigration altogether in the 1870s was that Prime Minister Sir John A. Macdonald feared that a labor shortage would jeopardize the deal under which British Columbia joined Confederation — the extension of the Canadian Pacific Railway to the Pacific Coast. Even then, Andrew Onderdonk, the American contractor building the B.C. portion of the line, had to assure the government that he would give white labor preference and would employ Indians and Chinese only if he could find no other workers in eastern Canada or elsewhere. But the young Yank apparently had his own agenda. Within a month of starting work, Onderdonk was hiring Chinese laborers recruited from San Francisco and Portland, Oregon, and in 1881, the first boatload of Chinese from Hong Kong came to toil on the CPR.

If we can believe the 1885 Royal Commission on Chinese Immigration, 15,701 Chinese entered Canada during the period from January, 1881, to June, 1884. Most of them left their wives and families behind, hoping to build a better life for them in Canada. They were sorely disappointed. Living conditions were miserable, medical assistance nonexistent, and the Chinese were paid only a dollar a day, one-half of what the whites were paid. Most of the newcomers were unprepared for the hardships of a Canadian winter. Many of the Chinese worked in the dangerous sections through the Rockies, for instance, drilling holes in chasm walls for explosives. The work took its toll. Conservative estimates are that 600 Chinese — or more than four men per mile — lost their lives working on the B.C. section of the CPR, through overwork, accident, disease and starvation. Yet not a single Chinese appears in the famous photograph of the last spike being driven for the CPR.

Once the railway was complete, cheap Chinese labor was suddenly no longer needed. "The people of B.C. now wanted them out because they were different, a threat, neither Christian nor white," concludes Graham Johnson, a University of British Columbia professor and author of *From China to Canada*. Their former bosses treated the Chinese with complete insensitivity, firing them on the spot and, in Pierre Berton's words, leaving them "to scrabble for pickings in the worked-out bars of the Fraser or to exist in near destitution in the dying towns along the completed track." On November 21, 1885, the Executive Council of British Columbia reported to the Secretary of State in Ottawa that "thousands of these people, having been summarily discharged by the railway contractors, and their earnings having been absorbed by their rapacious masters or owners, are now left in starving condition, and unless substantial relief be extended to them there is every prospect of their perishing during the winter."

Throughout the early 1880s, white British Columbians were stridently calling for the Dominion government to restrict Chinese immigration on the grounds that they took away jobs from Canadians and that they simply were not desirable. In 1885, Ottawa bowed to the incessant B.C. pressure and adopted Canada's first anti-Chinese bill, the shameful "head tax." This was a levy of $50 imposed upon virtually every person of Chinese origin entering the country. Even that wasn't enough to satisfy the B.C. politicians, who cajoled Ottawa into raising the tariff to $100 in 1890. And, in 1903, after a Royal Commission reported that the Chinese were paying little in the way of taxes and trying to avoid taxation whenever possible, it soared to

$500, which then represented about two years' wages for a Chinese Canadian worker. Ironically, this was going on at the same time as Ottawa was handing out cash and land to European settlers to settle the prairies. The excessive head taxes meant that it was simply too expensive for Chinese men to bring their wives and children across to Canada. As a result, the Chinatowns which sprouted up across the country were by-and-large communities of lonely bachelors. Estimates are that Ottawa collected $23 million from Chinese newcomers through the head tax. A century after the tax was first imposed, Chinese Canadians are still pressuring the federal government for some sort of compensation.

Throughout the late 1800s and early 1900s, union organizers and politicians used the Asian immigration question to win support among their constituents. According to University of Saskatchewan sociologist Peter Li, among the most notable was Noah Shakespeare, who formed the Anti-Chinese Association in 1879 and used Chinese exclusion as a plank in a platform that won him the Victoria mayor's office and later a seat as a member of Parliament. By 1880, all provincial political parties found it necessary to adopt anti-Chinese stances if they were to have any hope of winning elected office. Between 1884 and 1923, the British Columbia legislature passed numerous bills restricting the political and social rights of the Chinese, including legislation prohibiting them from acquiring Crown lands, holding a liquor licence, working as lawyers or pharmacists, or even having access to the provincial homes for the aged and infirm.

On Dominion Day, 1923, henceforth known by Chinese Canadians as Humiliation Day, MPs from British Columbia introduced the most repressive piece of legislation yet. The Chinese Immigration Act restricted entry into Canada to Chinese who were members of the diplomatic corps, Chinese children born in Canada, merchants and students. It also forced

Chinese immigrants to register with the Canadian government and to notify the government before leaving Canada temporarily, giving their foreign destination and the route they planned to follow. This act brought Chinese immigration in Canada to a virtual standstill.

These were tough years for Canada's Chinese. Despite their gradually declining numbers, they were still seen as an economic and racial threat, and their Chinatowns reviled as havens of immorality, infested with whorehouses, opium and gambling dens. Ironically, the Chinese lot in Canada only improved at the expense of Japanese Canadians, who were treated even worse by their adopted country, if such a thing is possible. When China emerged after the war as one of the victors over Japan, it became embarrassing for Canada to maintain a discriminatory policy toward a racial group of an allied country. By 1946, a committee for the repeal of the Chinese Immigration Act was formed which, by year's end, claimed support from most of Canada's newspapers, the Catholic and Protestant churches, the Council of Women, several members of Parliament and the Canadian Congress of Labor. In 1947, the same year that Canadians of Chinese and Indian origin were given the vote, the Chinese Immigration Act was finally repealed.

Sadly, though, the Chinese victory was more symbolic than real, and it was another twenty years before Chinese immigrants were finally placed on an equal footing with other nationalities. Prime Minister Mackenzie King set the tone for Canada's post-war immigration policy when, in May, 1947, he said in a speech to Parliament: "There will, I am sure, be general agreement with the view that the people of Canada do not wish, as a result of mass immigration, to make a fundamental alteration in the character of our population. Large-scale immigration from the Orient would change that fundamental composition of the Canadian population."

Since Canada's new laws allowed only the spouses of Chinese Canadians and their children to be admitted, some Chinese resorted to illegal immigration in the decade after 1947.

No one knows how many came into the country by illegal means. Even so, the RCMP launched a three-year investigation in 1959 which saw the offices of major Chinese organizations raided and documents seized. The politicians and the press, meanwhile, had a field day, claiming the immigration racket brought in $44 million in illegal profits over ten years.

But the Chinese community had learned much from their campaign to repeal the Chinese Immigration Act. They complained long and hard about their unfair treatment. Attempting to soothe the hurt, Ellen Fairclough, then Minister of Citizenship and Immigration, said in June, 1960, that it wasn't the government's intention to "prosecute or deport from the country any Chinese presently in Canada who have not themselves engaged in assisting other Chinese, apart from their own relatives, to enter Canada illegally." Soon after, she announced an amnesty program under which illegal Chinese immigrants could come forward and be allowed to stay in the country, provided they were "of sound moral character," and were not themselves engaged in illegal immigration. In the decade that followed, 11,569 Chinese came forward under the program, and as a result, gained legal status as Canadians.

By 1960, Ottawa had begun to think seriously about ways of ending the discriminatory features inherent in its immigration system. Two years later, a new era began when Ottawa finally altered its immigration rules to once-and-for-all eliminate discrimination on the basis of race or nationality. This meant that, for the first time since 1923, Chinese with no relatives in Canada could apply as independent immigrants.

But this wasn't as radical a shift in policy as it might appear. "Canada's immigration policy really is not a policy at all," argues Jamshed Mavalwala, an immigration expert at the University of Toronto. "It is a knee-jerk reaction to the events of the day." In the nineteenth century, remember, the federal government used generous land grants and financial handouts to sell prairie farming to Europeans. And, since the late 1960s, the federal government's main goal with its immigration policies has been to attract immigrants with the right skills and backgrounds to help stimulate the more-industrialized Canadian economy.

In fact, the true blueprint for what became Canada's business immigration policy is a 1966 federal White Paper which stressed the traditional reasons for encouraging immigration: population growth, expansion of the domestic market, lower per-capita costs of government and services, and cultural enrichment, while placing new emphasis on the importance of linking immigration policy to manpower factors, such as employment and productivity. The White Paper made a clear distinction between those immigrants who could compete in the economic marketplace and those who could not. That philosophy opened the door to what has become the great Hong Kong citizenship hustle.

The White Paper's findings sparked the introduction of important new elements into Canadian immigration law in 1967. The first was the federal government's "point system," through which independent immigrants were assessed under a number of criteria: education and training, occupation, location, age, knowledge of English and French, personal suitability and relatives living in Canada. Although still in use today, the point system has been altered many times. But the 1967 rules also allowed immigrants who wanted to set up businesses in Canada to apply as "entrepreneurs" — a sub-group under the independent immigrant category — provided they could show that they had sufficient funds to establish a viable business in Canada. In 1978, the Business Immigration Program was introduced, and business immigrants became a separate category within the Immigration Act for the first time. Applications from entrepreneurs were still given fourth priority in processing, after families trying to bring in relatives, refugees and selected workers.

Although business immigrants still had to qualify under the point system, they were now assessed mainly on their business skills. The criteria for entrance were relatively simple: the new business had to employ at least five Canadians other than the entrepreneur and dependants. The project had to make a significant contribution to the Canadian economy. And the entrepreneur had to be actively managing the business.

The savage recession of the early 1980s and concerns about increasingly high unemployment led to yet another re-examination of Canadian immigration policy. As a result, severe restrictions were placed on applicants in the "selected worker" category, and applicants in the independent class had to have a validated job offer in Canada before receiving a visa. But, predictably, business immigrants were exempt from both steps. In 1984 the Liberal government dramatically expanded the potential pool of business immigrants. Under the new rules, entrepreneurs now had to create only *one* new job rather than five. Potential business immigrants now jumped to third place in terms of priority when it came to being granted landed-immigrant status, ranking behind only family class and refugee immigrants. Moreover, applicants could now gain provisional admission which, incredibly, gave business people who could not even produce a business proposal up to two years to establish an enterprise which met all the necessary criteria.

But it was only after Brian Mulroney's Progressive Conservative party swept into power in 1984 that business immigration really took off. The Tories used the business classification as a weapon to strengthen the overall economy, create jobs and strengthen the economies of less-developed provinces. In the spring of 1985, a Progressive Conservative–dominated Parliamentary Standing Committee on Labour, Employment and Immigration reported that: "not enough attention has been paid to the potential for using immigration policy to facilitate economic and labor-market growth, to maintain, or enhance, current Canadian living standards for old and new Canadians, and to help smooth out economic and labor market fluctuations." The board also urged Parliament to "send a very clear signal to posts abroad that Canada nees jobs and is looking for their help in expanding the Entrepreneur Program."

Others involved in immigration take a more cynical view of the changes. William Yip, a Canadian-trained lawyer who now has a thriving practice in Hong Kong, says that what the government really wanted to do was import a class of skilled businessmen. Yip, a former member of the Ontario Liberal party, says that the Tories threw open the doors because, "Canadians are trained to be employees. The government wanted to bring in a new entrepreneurial class."

He may be right, because a year later, the Mulroney government launched the third, and most controversial element of the business immigration policy, one that some provincial trade officials in Hong Kong admit, off the record, amounts to little more than an exchange of cash for citizenship, at the ridiculously low price of $250,000 in booming Ontario, Quebec, Alberta and British Columbia, and $150,000 in less economically fortunate Saskatchewan, Manitoba, New Brunswick, Newfoundland, Prince Edward Island and Nova Scotia.

For several years, banks and other financial institutions had lobbied hard for a scheme that would allow foreign investors to plow money into Canadian ventures, with almost total anonymity. The banks in turn would do a booming business charging the would-be Canadians management fees, and would have a built-in layer of clients when they finally immigrated. In 1986, after a major selling effort by then immigration minister Walter McLean, Ottawa hatched a new "investor" category under the Business Immigration Program. This category was aimed at even wealthier foreigners than those who qualified for the entrepreneurial program. To gain admission as an investor, immigrants did not even have to actively manage a business. All the newcomers needed to have was a personal net worth of

$500,000 or more, and commit at least $250,000, or $150,000 depending on where in Canada the money was headed, for a minimum of three years, to an investment that would contribute to business development and job creation. Investors could directly invest their cash in a particular business. Or they could leave the work of managing their money in the hands of one of the dozens of investment syndicates, or government-sponsored venture-capital funds, which popped up to accommodate the millions in foreign cash.

Ottawa however was a stickler on one point: an investor must have acquired his money "through his own efforts." Early on, that subtle distinction was lost on many clan patriarchs back in Hong Kong, who did not understand that they cannot simply give a son or daughter enough money to qualify for the investor category and expect the children to be automatically accepted by Canadian immigration officials.

Their initial confusion was understandable. After all, if most of the investor money is passive and managed entirely by a registered syndicate, why does it matter whose money it is? The problem, of course, is entirely political. Says Edward Hung, a Toronto criminal and immigration lawyer who was born in Hong Kong: "It seems clear that the government doesn't want to sound like all Canada wants is the money."

The program got off to a bad start in Hong Kong when a few Alberta businessmen — and Ontario entrepreneurs working through Alberta — tried to sell projects without clearing them with the Hong Kong Securities Commission. Ontario initially had strong reservations about the whole thing, partly because of the Alberta kerfuffle, partly because they thought that the federal government had gone about it in a half-cocked way, and partly because of the passive nature of the investments. Other critics labeled the investor category an undisguised attempt to sell visas to high-rollers — at the expense of other immigration classes. But that argument was lost on McLean, for one, who insisted that the program complemented, but did not compete with the other existing immigration categories.

Even so, the program drew increased fire when the fund managers decided they wanted to be able to provide guarantees for the investments, which would make it even easier for them to hustle citizenship for cash in Hong Kong. In 1987 the funds began lobbying provincial governments to take their case to Ottawa. While Ottawa was at first cool, things really began to heat up when Quebec officials found a loophole in the regulations and decided that it was within their jurisdiction to offer investment guarantees. They instructed several Quebec investment firms to put together investment packages for immigrant investors which were fully guaranteed by the provincial government, and on top of that, the Quebec government even added a new, lucrative element to the citizenship hustle, by paying investors an annual interest rate of 3 to 4 per cent on their $250,000 gamble.

A nasty intergovernmental row ensued. In response to Quebec's move, Immigration Canada put final processing of investor applications on hold until the province and federal government could reach an agreement. Quebec premier Robert Bourassa was drawn into the battle when he called Prime Minister Brian Mulroney, asking him to intervene and resolve the dispute in the province's favor. Ultimately, the federal government bowed to the pressure. In April, 1988, Ottawa expanded the guidelines for eligibility under the investor immigration program to include a new "three-tier" system. Under the new rules, investments that are guaranteed by a third party are also eligible. But the applicant must have a net worth of $700,000 and make a minimum investment of $500,000, which is then locked in for five years instead of three. "It may sound like trickles, but it adds up to rivers," says Louis Ferguson. "The idea is to obtain financing for small or medium-sized enterprises which the provinces consider important to their regional economic development. Traditional financial institutions just are not willing to make loans to these people."

But even that wasn't enough for Quebec which held up the passage of the legislation because it wasn't to be included among the list of "have not" provinces, where investors can qualify for admission by investing just $150,000 for three years. Today, while investors have the option of applying individually for investor status, professionally managed syndicates are the slick fast track to Canadian citizenship. The process can take several forms, but at its simplest applicants write out a cheque for $150,000 or $250,000 — depending upon where the fund is based — make a formal application at the Canadian visa office in Hong Kong, complete a medical examination, undergo a security review, and wait. If a visa is granted, the investors are free to live where they want; if entrance is refused, either for medical or security reasons, the fund simply returns the cash to the investor.

The most common type of fund pools together cash from a dozen-or-so Hong Kong investors and re-invests it in a constantly changing list of stocks, preferred shares or bonds in eligible projects and businesses. But there are also more specific funds which funnel the money into a particular project, or development, which has been approved by the federal and provincial governments. These include everything from hotels and real estate to high-tech companies.

The fund managers prepare an offering document which must be cleared by the various provincial regulatory authorities. To qualify, the funds must satisfy the conditions of the Immigration Act, which means that the investments must result in significant economic benefit to Canada by creating jobs and contributing to economic expansion.

The funds must also fit the province's economic priorities. In British Columbia, for instance, funds can qualify by investing in everything from manufacturing, scientific research and development and tourism, to information processing, feature films, aquaculture or shopping centre development. About all that is unacceptable in B.C. is investing in single- and multiple-family residential real estate, and importing operations. More selective is Ontario, which stresses manufacturing projects as well as projects to be located in smaller communities outside of the so-called Golden Triangle in the southern part of the province. Meanwhile, Prince Edward Island encourages firms to set up businesses which are involved in food processing, fishing and agriculture, craft design and production, high-technology manufacturing and manufacturing health care products.

Now in its third year, the investor program is starting to gather steam. Only 153 business immigrants entered Canada under its aegis in 1987, 53 of them from Hong Kong. But during 1988, 245 investor immigrants entered Canada, 107 from Hong Kong. Prospective immigrants have around a hundred syndicates or funds to choose from. Many fund managers, who are usually paid an annual percentage of the fund's assets under management, plus an investment fee based on the fund's performance, have become very, very rich. The most successful have been those organizations with the energy and financial clout to peddle their products aggressively in Hong Kong. Canadian banks, led by investor-fund pioneer, the Canadian Imperial Bank of Commerce, are particularly bullish in the burgeoning citizenship-for-cash sector. So is the Canadian Maple Leaf Fund Ltd., managed by First Generation Resources Ltd., a Vancouver-based investment company which is the biggest of them all, with $30 million in cash, most of it flowing from Hong Kong. Chairman Steven Funk attributes this success to the fact that they are the only fund with a full-time office in Hong Kong. It is headed by Wilson Ng, a ten-year veteran of the Canadian High Commission in Hong Kong who meets with potential investors on an one-by-one basis. First Generation also has hired hands on site in Taipei, Manila and London, England.

Another big player is the Merbanco Group, Calgary's first merchant-banking operation, which runs a total of seven funds in Alberta, Vancouver and Saskatchewan and has $27 million in assets. Says Merbanco president Robert Wisener, who cut his teeth in the venture-capital world by marrying western Canadian resources to eastern Canadian money during the booming oil and natural gas market of the 1970s: "We are just starting to probe this market." Exactly how big could the passport-for-cash market become? First Generation's Steven Funk thinks that it has the potential to grown to a staggering $500 million a year as 1997 nears.

Despite all the refinements and apparent checks and balances in the system, there are many Canadians, Chinese and non-Chinese alike, who think that the Progressive Conservative government has sacrificed the integrity of Canada's immigration program in a blatant grab for the colony's wealthiest citizens. Critics also complain that the program simply allows wealthy business people to leapfrog the lineups to get ahead of more traditional immigrants: family members, skilled workers and refugees. They say that the program is tantamount to selling passports, and accuse the government of creating an elitist immigration program for the well-heeled. At the very least, there is a strong feeling that the emphasis on attracting entrepreneurs and investors delays processing of the other immigration categories. Says Dan Heap, the federal New Democratic Party immigration critic, and a member of a parliamentary committee which examined Canada's immigration policy: "It used to be that family reunification and aiding refugees were the cornerstones of Canada's immigration system. But under the Tories the main goal has been bringing in foreign businessmen and investors, which is entirely in keeping with the Mulroney government's view that money — not people — makes the world go around."

Ottawa's biggest embarrassment has been its own inept management of the program. While Ferguson and his department are exasperated by doubters, and trumpet those impressive

Hong Kong investment and job creation numbers over and over, the truth is that the bureaucrats really don't know how well the system works because they can't keep track of either investment cash or money. As Victor Malarek recounted in his book, *Heaven's Gates*, suspicions that the investment and job creation figures attributed to business immigrants could be exaggerated first surfaced in the spring of 1985, after the House of Commons Standing Committee on Labour, Employment and Immigration urged Ottawa to open the floodgates further for business immigrants. In May, 1985, Gaétan Lussier, deputy-minister and chairman of the Canadian Employment and Immigration Commission, launched an enquiry into the validity of Immigration Canada's grand claims for the program. The findings were extremely disturbing: "It became clear from that enquiry that there exists no systematic tracking capability, and that, on the whole, there is inadequate information on what happens to all entrepreneurs admitted to Canada." The confidential government study, prepared by Employment and Immigration Canada's Strategic Policy and Planning Branch, concluded that most monitoring efforts were highly selective and that notable, and incredible, gaps exist in British Columbia and Quebec. "In short, the economic benefits attributed to the Entrepreneur Program are based solely upon the declared intentions of the successful applicants."

The truth is that once these entrepreneurs gain entrance into Canada, the government really has no idea where they go or what they do. The team which conducted the study could not even locate 395, or, more than one-third, of the 1,056 Hong Kong businessmen in the sample group. The worst showing was in Montreal, where 225 of 351 entrepreneurs could not be found to be interviewed. It turned out that wealthy immigrants from Hong Kong and Taiwan had long been using Quebec, which operates one of the most aggressive recruitment offices in Hong Kong, as a springboard to settle elsewhere in Canada — usually Toronto. Of the 661 the investigators were able to track down across the country, another 308 entrepreneurs did not take part in the survey because they were either away or simply refused to discuss their activities. As a result, only 353 were questioned. Out of that sample, 272 respondents, or 77 per cent, had an ongoing established business. But, even then, less capital was being transferred to Canada than originally indicated. Likewise, the majority of entrepreneurs were also unable to create as many jobs as they had originally promised.

Embarassed by the revelations, the then minister of state for Immigration, Walter McLean, announced in 1986 that the Immigration department would implement stricter controls on entrance and monitoring and begin granting only conditional visas. This would give immigrants two years in which to get their businesses going. But just two years later, Jack Hughes, a rosy-cheeked, pleasant senior official with the Business Immigration section of Ontario's Ministry of Industry, Trade and Technology, still professed a sense of helplessness in coping with the overwhelming volume of Hong Kong traffic into Canada: "There are an awful lot of very marginal cases. But we have never been given the manpower to check them out. We do not know what they are doing once they get here."

Even the fictional detective Sam Spade would have a tough time gleaning information about several garment manufacturers who are said to conduct business at 215 Spadina Avenue, a nondescript low-rise in the heart of Toronto's Chinatown where even the residents of the building seem not to know who their neighbors are. Upstairs, the various company names are written on paper or cardboard and tacked to the door frames, giving the impression of temporary residence, at best. Many of the rooms have two or three small religious shrines at their entrance, or just inside the main factory space, where the workers make offerings of tea and fruit, and where, on the first and fifteenth of the month, a whole pig is often barbecued.

The Ontario Ministry of Industry and Trade's records show that Annley Fashions, one of the registered tenants of the building, received $200,000 from Hong Kong investors to retain five jobs and create six more. Inside the fifth-floor loft space, which is supposed to house Annley's operations, two rows of seamstresses are hidden behind piles of padded coat material. The women range in age from eighteen to more than sixty, all of them hard at work forcing the thick material through sewing machines. To alleviate boredom, a rock music station blares popular music above the roar of the machines.

The main decoration in the room is a large aquarium strategically located to attract bad luck in which big orange and black fish swim lazily in scummy water. The clothing racks are filled with row upon row of finished dressing gowns and sets of purple floral beach pants and tops. No one seems to be able to find the owner and manager, a man named Danny Chu. A woman hollers down the freight elevator in Chinese and a male voice barks back, but the owner of the voice fails to appear. Ten minutes later the woman leads the way to the freight entrance outside where a man identified as Chu and a group of Chinese men are loading material from the back of a van into an elevator. When asked about the project's Hong Kong investors — Kit Ling, Romy Leung and Siu Yau Ma — Chu is evasive and says to return at 5:00 P.M., but, at 5:00 P.M. Chu is nowhere in sight. After several telephone calls, one of the employees finally locates him. But Chu says that there has been a mistake and that Annley Fashions moved out of the building months ago. When asked about the fact that he recognized the names of Leung and Ma, the investors, Chu simply hangs up, and disappears back into the cracks of Ottawa's poorly administered Business Immigration Program.

Even Louis Ferguson, the man responsible for the program, admits that there are still cracks in the system which Ottawa is trying to plug. Ferguson says that part of the problem is that there is simply little the government can do to force recalcitrant entrepreneurs to live up to their commitments. Under the Immigration Act, a person is not guaranteed the right to remain in the country simply because he has been granted landed-immigrant status. He can lose his visa, particularly if it was conditional upon fulfilling job-creation and investment criteria. But as of November, 1988, Ottawa had expelled few business immigrants for failing to meet visa conditions. Ferguson, however, is unapologetic about Ottawa's reluctance to act. "This isn't a police state," he said. "The idea is to make sure you do your work on the front end to ensure that the entrants are well-qualified."

By summer 1989, Ottawa had developed an elaborate computer system to keep track of the program and its participants.

But shoddy monitoring is really only the tip of Ottawa's problems. Regional development was one of the government's stated goals in launching the Business Immigration Program back in 1978. The idea was that business immigration would be a useful tool for stimulating some of the underdeveloped regions of Canada. It has not worked. From 1981, when the program really got going, through the end of 1986, an average of 39 per cent of the business immigrants destined for Canada each year ended up in Ontario, 25 per cent in Quebec and 20 per cent in British Columbia. Only 5 per cent headed to Manitoba, and less than 2 per cent for Saskatchewan. Faring even worse were the four Atlantic provinces, the Northwest Territories and the Yukon. Altogether, they received less than 3 per cent of the annual business immigrants to Canada.

After looking at those figures in late 1987, Alan Nash, a research associate with the Ottawa-based Institute for Research on Public Policy, concluded that if the pattern persists, business immigration could actually aggravate the problem by accelerating the very economic differences which regional development programs have been trying to reduce. "Moreover," he reported, "the situation is worse than it appears, because entrepreneur immigration is so concentrated in Montreal, Toronto and Vancouver. Thus, even within the provinces that receive the largest

amounts of funds, the program exacerbates regional development problems."

To be fair, Ottawa isn't entirely to blame. Ostensibly, the
program is a federal operation. But the provinces really call the
shots when it comes to determining what funds and projects
qualify. A prospective enterpreneurial immigrant first submits a
business proposal to the federal visa officer abroad, who passes it
on to the appropriate province back in Canada, or provincial
office in Hong Kong, for advice. The provinces set their own
requirements. These can include such information as financial
statements, cash-flow forecasts, market research and projec-
tions and competitor information. A documented statement of
personal net worth, and proof of ability to transfer funds, are
also required as part of the application. But those qualifications
are easily met by Hong Kong's wealthy citizens.

The growing wave of Hong Kong money is causing fierce
interprovincial competition. Alberta, which has long sought to
diversify its economy away from oil and gas development, was
one of the first provinces to open a trade office in Hong Kong, in
1980. It spent more than $1 million to run its office in 1987 after
Li Ka-shing's high-profile investment in Husky Oil. Following
quickly on Alberta's heels was British Columbia. But, ironically,
B.C., which is attracting thousands of Hong Kong residents,
operates one of the quieter provincial offices in the colony.

Publicly the government of Ontario, which has just one full-
time Canadian agent and three locals on its Hong Kong staff,
says that it doesn't actively recruit applicants for the Business
Immigration Program. But Barton Hildebrand, director of the
Investment and Regional Operations Branch of the Ontario
Ministry of Industry, Trade and Technology, said that his office
is planning to increase exposure in Hong Kong.

By far the biggest push is coming from Quebec which maintains an operation in one of Hong Kong's most prestigious
addresses: the futuristic twin blue-glass towers of the Bond
Centre. There, Quebec officials gaze out over the teeming Hong

Kong harbor and dream of luring some of the colony's wealthiest citizens to their province. Quebec also reaps the benefits of the Montreal Urban Community's (MUC) Hong Kong office. *La belle province* has a big advantage over the competition. A 1978 agreement between Quebec and Ottawa, the Cullen–Coulture Agreement, gives the province more say than other provinces in the selection of immigrants. Quebec, in fact, can even admit immigrants who do not meet the federal government selection criteria, so long as they are not rejected on security or medical grounds.

Quebec has exercised its unique powers often enough to gain a reputation as the "back door to Canada" among Hong Kong businessmen. If you can't get by the feds, the advice in Hong Kong is to go to Quebec. In 1983, just 21 per cent of the business immigrants to Canada moved to Quebec. By 1988, 40 per cent of immigrants arriving from abroad headed for Quebec. Just how long they stayed there is very much open to question.

The figures are grossly misleading. As Immigration Canada's own study indicated, hundreds of wealthy Asian immigrants, armed with their special visas, never even make it to Quebec. Instead, they simply change airplanes in Montreal and head for Toronto or Vancouver. That means that the impact of these newcomers on the Quebec economy is limited. Quebec's Department of Immigration simply says that it is Ottawa's job to monitor the business immigrants. But Quebec's role as an underground railroad from Asia to Canada is likely to grow, particularly since Premier Robert Bourassa's tough stand on language rights has turned off many potential Chinese immigrants. "The Hong Kongers are very sensitive to political stability," says Toronto realtor Edward Hou. "They have just come from one shaky country and they don't want to move into another unstable situation."

That perception troubles Quebec officials, and often causes them to spend long hours brooding over drinks in their favorite haunt, the Hong Kong Foreign Correspondents Club. They were particularly upset in December, 1988, when the Supreme Court of Canada ruled that Quebec's French-only sign law was illegal. Just days before the ruling, Hong Kong's major English-language newspaper, *The South China Morning Post*, ran an article which warned potential visitors to the province not to travel there on the day of the Supreme Court ruling. Bourassa, said the article, had appealed for calm on the day of the decision. The upshot of the article was clear in the minds of Quebec officials: lack of political stability would kill off investment negotiations with some of Hong Kong's wealthiest citizens.

Canada's provinces are not just competing with each other. Other countries are also trying to capitalize on Hong Kong's economic uncertainty. In 1982, Australia launched a program, very similar to Canada's, that requires foreign entrepreneurs to transfer $500,000 (Australian) in exchange for landed immigrant status. The goals of the program are to create and retain jobs, introduce new technology and stimulate exports and reduce imports. Thanks to an aggressive advertising and promotional drive, Australia issued 370 visas under its Business Migrant Program in 1984-85, which increased to 456 in 1985-86 and 919 in 1986-87. About 40 per cent of the immigrants came from Hong Kong.

After looking at the Australian program, Alan Nash of the Institute for Research on Public Policy, concluded that it suffered from the same problems as the Canadian equivalent: considerable regional disparity resulting from the destinations chosen by business migrants; and an inability by the government to ensure that business migrants comply with program objectives.

But, thanks to some expressions of profound racism, the Aussie program may already be losing steam. In 1988, Asian immigration had emerged as a touchy political issue in Australia. Public opinion polls in the summer of 1988 showed that huge majorities were in favor of choking off the flow. Slogans such as

"Asians out" started to appear on roadside rocks on the New South Wales coast, and radio phone-in shows confirmed the rise in racism. Among local Vietnamese, Chinese and Japanese populations, there was deepening anxiety about the debate. And abroad, in places like Hong Kong, where Australia's redneck outbursts were widely reported in the press, Australia's attractiveness as a potential new home and safe haven plummeted. Says Alan Nash: "Among Hong Kong citizens, Australia is still very much viewed as a racist country."

In future, however, Canada's toughest competitor could be the United States, which would be the first choice of many people leaving Hong Kong if it were easier to enter. Many U.S. business people in Hong Kong have long looked with envy at the popularity of the Canadian Business Immigration Program. An anonymous U.S. diplomat in Hong Kong complained that Canadians "were not playing fair," and accused Canada of skimming off some of the brightest stars in the nervous colony. The American bureaucrat failed to mention the U.S. government's own attempts to woo wealthy Hong Kong residents. Prior to October 1, 1987, there was a quota on Hong Kong–born immigrants admitted to the United States each year. In March, 1988, the U.S. Senate passed an immigration bill which included a program similar to Canada's own entrepreneurial immigration program. The new U.S. legislation requires foreign entrepreneurs to spend the equivalent of $2.5 million (CDN) and create ten jobs in exchange for a conditional visa.

For the moment, however, the biggest problems facing the men and women who run Canada's Business Immigration Program may be closer to home, as the Australian disease takes root in this country. The bureaucrats are well aware that the political bosses who dictate the country's immigration policies can sour on business immigration just as quickly as they embraced it. After all, public opinion, along with economic goals, have historically been the major factors in determining federal immigration policy. By early 1989, a public backlash against business immigration had already begun as more and more attention focused on the rich Asians coming into Canada.

Emotions are running the highest in British Columbia, where residents blame Hong Kong immigrants for everything from skyrocketing house prices to overcrowded schools and dramatically changing neighborhoods. A poll conducted by the *Vancouver Sun* in November, 1988, found that 70 per cent of mainland Vancouver Island residents thought that immigration laws should be tightened, while more than 70 per cent of people surveyed said that the main source-countries for immigrants should be Western Europe, Britain, and Eastern Europe rather than other countries. Their inability to deal with the questions of real estate speculation and lack of affordable housing has already cost B.C.'s Social Credit government one seat. And a group speaking out against Asian newcomers, the British-European Immigration Aid Foundation, has been formed to fight Canada's immigration laws, which it says are threatening Canada's British and European character. The British Columbia government has already clicked on its damage control systems by making the provincial immigration incentives even more enticing, while at the same time trying to encourage Asian immigrants to settle in the sparsely populated wilds of British Columbia, far from the leafy suburbs of Vancouver.

Meanwhile, the pressure on Ottawa continues to grow as bags of mail denouncing the program, some with a particularly racist tone, have started to pile up in Department of Immigration offices in Ottawa. Said one federal immigration official: "Once too many non-whites start coming in, most Canadians start to get nervous." Ultimately, the program's future may hang upon whether the economic benefits of bringing in monied foreigners are enough to outweigh deepening public opposition. The cynical among us might conclude that the real question is: with which policy do the governments think they can obtain the most votes? In any event, the drama is only beginning to unfold. The true test will come when the stream of Hong Kong immigrants turns into a flood.

5/ TORONTO:
A CITY FOR
THE TAKING

They arrive at Toronto's Lester B. Pearson International Airport in small, sober, conservatively dressed groups; only their Rolex watches and glittering diamond rings hint at their wealth. No sooner do they complete landing formalities than they are led to limousines or spacious mini-vans that whisk them off to the city. These men and women are representatives of some of the richest and most powerful families of Hong Kong, Taiwan and Singapore. They are on a shopping trip of sorts. But, instead of trendy Yorkville or Eaton Centre merchandise, they are scouting for houses, office towers, condominium blocks, shopping malls and any garment factories, restaurants or other thriving businesses which might be up for sale. They do not stay for long, sometimes measuring their visits in mere hours rather than days. Yet, by the time they leave, the wealthy visitors will often have spent millions of dollars on buying spree that might include a palatial family home, a string of condominiums which may sit empty for months, a strip shopping mall in a Toronto suburb and an office tower near one of the city's burgeoning

Chinatowns. They are transforming Toronto's downtown sky-
lines and neighborhoods, and even altering the orderly, conservative city's WASPish social fabric.

As 1997 approaches, the freewheeling capitalists of Hong
Kong are pouring money into Canada's richest, most important
city, at a staggering rate. Each year it is estimated that Hong
Kong businessmen spend $2 to $3 billion on Toronto condos,
apartment and office buildings and shopping malls. That figure
doesn't even take into account the investments made by hus-
tling entrepreneurs who have set up everything from high-
technology companies to garment factories, all bankrolled by
Hong Kong money. Nor does it include the other assets being
shifted into the city.

Suddenly, Hong Kong money, and the men and women who
wield it, seem to be everywhere in Toronto. Most of the city's
300,000 Chinese still make their homes near the city's downtown Chinatown. This older Chinatown presents to the visitor
a startling panorama of incongruous architecture, teeming capitalism and ancestral poverty that stand in colorful contrast to
the city that surrounds it. But the affluent northeastern neighborhood of Agincourt has also become a "Little China." Today,
roughly 40 per cent of Toronto's Chinese community live in the
area, unofficially referred to as "Asiancourt," which has its own
ornate, Chinese-style shopping malls, restaurants, cinemas and
entertainment spots. One of the most popular nightspots imports singers from the Orient to entertain the well-dressed,
cellular phone–toting crowd with Chinese pop songs as well as
Cantonese versions of North American hits. Those who can't
afford Agincourt can opt for the smaller, downmarket enclave
in the vicinity of Broadview Avenue and Gerrard Street. And
another Chinatown is already sprouting up in the sprawling,
West Toronto suburb of Mississauga.

The monied newcomers have even penetrated, the city's —
and therefore, Canada's — old-money establishment. For decades, Toronto's exclusive Bridle Path area has been home to

pillars of Canadian business like the Bassetts, Westons, and Blacks. But these days it is also home to the Au-Yeungs, Fungs, Hos, Luks and Chows. Not to mention the Wus, Vongs, Cheungs and Longs. Green, leafy streets such as Post Road, The Bridle Path and High Point Road are now sprinkled with homes owned by recent immigrants from Hong Kong's middle and upper class. In fact, it is estimated that one in every six houses on High Point Road is owned by a Hong Kong family.

The two disparate cultures do not mix easily. Among the Tudor manors, French *châteaux* and 1960s geometric experiments now stand ornate marble-and-stucco structures with snarling Oriental stone lions at the gates. And, between the tennis courts and putting-green lawns are back yards where tiny Oriental bridges allow the owners to cross rippling streams.

Many of the older residents have never spoken to the new families from Hong Kong. Their explanation is that the area's two-to-fourteen acre properties are simply so large that they never meet them. (The Bridle Path is probably the only neighborhood in Canada where a municipal by-law stipulates that no lot can be smaller than two acres.) But there is more to it than that. The Hong Kong people themselves freely admit that they are partly to blame for the lack of rapport between the two cultures. "People in the Asian rim don't communicate with their neighbors," says one recent newcomer. "The culture is to care about your own business and nothing beyond that. We see people as an obstacle, a bother, even if they want to help us. In Hong Kong people have lost that human touch. They stay at home more and concentrate on family life. In Canada we should communicate more." Only recently have Chinese home owners started to appear at the neighborhood's ratepayers' association meetings, according to Alex Fisher, past president of the association and a resident of the area for more than thirty years. Says Fisher: "At first they were reticent about coming out. But now some have even paid association dues. I think that more and more they are beginning to feel that they are welcome as neighbors."

Even so, there is an undercurrent of suspicion among some residents as more Chinese faces appear at the neighborhood plaza, the local private school, and real estate open houses. Said one mother, who lives on High Point Road in a house that faces a row of four Chinese-owned houses: "My kids have trouble at Crescent School because they see the Chinese and the East Indian kids get the most awards. My daughter came home and said that maybe I should give more money to the school because those kids get all the parts in the plays. A friend of mine was going to take her child out of Bayview Glen because of the high numbers of Chinese there. I am not against them coming to Canada. But it is like they are taking over everything."

Even more alarmed is Marion Colapinto, who has called The Bridle Path home for twenty years. "There have been a lot more Chinese buyers in the past two and a half years. And there are perfectly charming homes that have been trashed by them to put up great abortions. I have no racist feelings, but they have so much money it is kind of scary. When we moved here in the 1960s, kids played on the street and you could run next door to borrow a cup of sugar. Now people are very hesitant."

This tide of alien opulence may breed envy and resentment among some members of the city's old-money club. But any who long for the good old days are likely do so only within the comfort of their mansions. Money, as the denizens of The Bridle Path well know, opens doors. Toronto, it is clear, is welcoming Hong Kong money with open arms. Asian expatriates are now playing a prominent role in all aspects of Toronto public life, people like Robert Wong, a second-generation Chinese Canadian who holds down the powerful Energy, Mines and Resources portfolio in Ontario's Liberal government and high-powered Toronto school board trustee Olivia Chow, who married Toronto city councillor Jack Layton in 1988. At the same time, groups such as Toronto's five-year-old Chinese Businesswomen's Executive Network, which introduces Chinese women to business contacts and holds seminars on practical matters like family law and tax reform, attest to the city's thriving immigrant community. So does the Charity Through Fashion fund-raiser which was held in September, 1988. This was the first time that the Chinese community and the non-Chinese community came together in Toronto for a major fund-raising event. "Before, there was a perception that we Chinese in Canada are selfish, looking after ourselves and opening up only to our families," billionaire Stanley Ho said in Cantonese to those present at the $350-a-head event, a crowd sprinkled with dignitaries from Canada's business community, including the chairman of the Bank of Nova Scotia and federal finance minister Michael Wilson. "But today we are showing that Hong Kong people support going into the broader community."

Another vivid sign of the affluence — and influence — of the city's newly established Oriental entrepreneurs was Noble House, an elite but short-lived country club in Agincourt, which subsequently went out of business. Among those present at the July 5, 1987, gala opening of the club: Prime Minister Brian Mulroney, finance minister Michael Wilson, and a thousand of the city's business people who listened and talked business as a taut jazz trio greased the wheels of commerce in the club's gigantic ballroom.

Then, there's the Mandarin Club, which reputedly serves the city's best Cantonese cuisine, atop the large Dragon City shopping mall at the corner of Spadina Avenue and Dundas Street, in the heart of old Chinatown. Each day, Bay Street's upper crust rubs shoulders with Hong Kong immigrants in the club's elegant meeting rooms, where jade-green carpeting and hand-painted vases provide a serene Eastern atmosphere. On weekends there are social events, but during the week it is business that keeps the club running at near capacity. Membership is by invitation only. And, while there are no restrictions on females or non-Chinese members, it probably helps if you have money. The $1,200 initiation fee and annual dues of about $600 also provide guest privileges at Hong Kong's exclusive Kowloon Club. About 60 per cent of the Mandarin's 500 members emigrated from Hong Kong within the past six years; 25 per cent are long-established Chinese Canadians; and about 15 per cent are Caucasian Bay Streeters. Among the Caucasian members are officials from the Royal Bank of Canada, HongKong Bank of Canada and Canadian Imperial Bank of Commerce. The club's original list of honorary co-chairmen reflects the club's striking cultural duality. It included former Ontario Lieutenant-Governor John Black Aird and Michael O. Sanderson, the high-profile president of Merrill Lynch Canada Inc., one of Canada's leading brokerage houses, as well as Cheng Yu-tung, the head of Hong Kong–based New World Hotels (during 1987, the top revenue–producing company in the colony) and Ronald Fook-Shiu Li, another of the colony's mega-rich.

In fact, if there is a single metaphor for what Hong Kong money is doing to Toronto, none is better than the Mandarin Club and the $18-million Dragon City mall which houses it. When a beautiful deserted Hungarian Catholic church was knocked down in 1986 to build the mall, with its 180,000 square feet of retail, office, apartment and parking space, it symbolized the eclipse of the old European immigrant community that once dominated Spadina Avenue and the Kensington Market area.

In truth, the Chinese have been coming to Toronto ever since the first hand-laundry opened on Adelaide Street more than a century ago. Indeed, the first Chinese immigrants to Ontario arrived before the completion of the CPR in 1887, probably traveling by way of the United States. The pioneers were not made welcome in Anglo-Saxon Toronto. The unions spearheaded anti-Chinese sentiment. In December, 1883, for example, the Canadian Labour Congress met in Dufferin Hall in Toronto, where its newly elected president urged the delegates to pay heed to the "Chinese immigration curse." The issue was Chinese laundries and one delegate complained that "Christian people in Toronto would hire Chinese to do their washing" before they would hire "the poor white woman who had a family to support." He added that the Chinese could be "starved out of Toronto, notwithstanding the large number of rats and cats in the city." A 1914 Ontario law stipulated that "no Chinese person shall employ in any capacity or have under his direction or control any female white person in factory, restaurant or laundry."

Despite the widespread racial discrimination, the Chinese community expanded rapidly, and by 1910, 1,000 of the province's 2,800 recorded Chinese made their homes in Toronto. The growing community included the owners of many wholesale businesses, groceries and restaurants. And, by 1910, a Chinatown section of the city was identifiable for the first time around the downtown intersection of King and Queen streets. Yet, all the while, white hostility to Chinatown grew, fed by lurid accounts of opium and white-slave traffic, and assertions in publications such as *Maclean's, Saturday Night* and the muckracking newspaper *Jack Canuck* that Orientals were inferior to Anglo-Saxons.

The Chinese Immigration Act of 1923 effectively ended the growth of Toronto's Chinese community for the next twenty-five years. In the late 1930s, deaths and departures reduced the Chinese population to the point where there were predictions that the community could disappear altogether, in Toronto and even in the country as a whole. But, beginning in 1950, the numbers of Chinese immigrants began to increase. After 1967, the flow increased sharply.

Toronto gained an increasing share of the new immigrants, largely because of the better job opportunities in thriving southern Ontario. By the mid-1970s, the largest Canadian Chinese community was in Toronto. Moreover, the Hong Kong connection was already well-established. There had been no direct migration at all from China to Canada from 1949 until 1974. Thus, the vast majority of new immigrants came by way of Hong Kong, where they had become accustomed to urban life, and, in many cases, had learned to write and speak English.

Still, there was change. Most of the city's original Chinatown, in the vicinity of Bay and Queen streets, was razed to make way for the new City Hall more than two decades ago, but a new Chinatown quickly developed farther west, with Dundas and Spadina as its hub. And today, the old and new Chinatowns have converged, both literally and figuratively.

Walk along Dundas from Yonge Street toward Spadina and watch Toronto's conservative surroundings dissolve in an exotic caldron of swarming crowds, chattering voices, startling sights and greasy, tantalizing scents which would make even the loneliest Hong Konger feel that he had never left home. Garish banners, placards and signs bearing elaborate Cantonese script criss-cross building facades. Tanks full of lobsters and rows of glistening ducks can be seen in dusty, grease-smeared windows. Gigantic, carved lions and dragons guard the entrances to fantastic crimson, gold and jade restaurants where diners gulp down bowls of steaming, Szechuan-, Mandarin- and Cantonese-style food. Inside crowded stores, animated, white-coated barkers peddle spices and oils, fruits and vegetables, and sticky cakes and sweets. Its signal lights flashing, a silver Mercedes-Benz sits on the sidewalk as several Chinese men unload boxes from its trunk. Jackhammers noisily punch holes in the pavement of the site of what will soon be a large shopping mall. Herbalists and practitioners of acupuncture advertise treatments that will cure "rheumatism, insomnia, allergy, headaches, menoxenia, skin diseases," and help sufferers to "quit smoking and lose weight."

Maneuvering through the crowded streets, you pass a short, wizened man and sturdy woman, both of indeterminable age, carrying plastic bags full of groceries. Beside them, a trio of clean-cut, North Americanized Chinese teenagers, sporting Beaver Canoe sweatshirts, topsiders and Walkman radios, laugh and talk in accented English. A well-off Chinese couple in their early thirties, their faces reflecting the softness of high-living, pushes arrogantly through the crowd. In a nearby doorway, a knot of wiry, leather-jacketed young toughs, their hair sculpted into Elvis pompadours, draw on cigarettes and glare a challenge at anyone who dares to look their way.

Today's Chinatown is as much a place of new wealth as old tradition. You can see it in Dragon City, the futuristic complex made of glass and brick on the corner of Dundas and Spadina. Henry and Daniel Hung, both still in their thirties, used their Hong Kong family's money to bankroll their grandiose plans. Or, moving south on Spadina, you can see wealth and tradition combined in the $35-million Chinatown Centre, which is being developed by Manbro Developments, also with Hong Kong money.

The colony's vast wealth has also found a haven in the colorful restaurants that line Spadina, some of which employ as many as a hundred people. Patrick Chan, who immigrated from Hong Kong in the 1960s to work for a Toronto currency trading firm, owns one of Chinatown's largest restaurants, the Chinatown International Chinese Restaurant. The International, which can seat 500 people or host two wedding banquets at the same time, and has a foot-high dilapidated red shrine near the front door and a garish pink chandelier hanging in the main foyer, is one of the preferred venues for the Chinatown equivalent of the power lunch. Here, well-dressed men hammer out deals to buy and sell office towers and condominium blocks, pausing only when interrupted by women pushing trollies of steaming pork-filled dumplings, crispy duck and spun-sugar apples and bananas.

Nearby is the huge Hsin Kuang restaurant: a forbidding, windowless, yellow-brick building with the largest illuminated sign on Spadina, and two large stone lions on pedestals that dare you to enter the front door. The Hsin Kuang is part of a chain of Cantonese restaurants launched by a group of independent businessmen in Hong Kong in 1980. Four years later, they decided it was time to expand into Canada, so nine of the partners — dubbed "the pioneers" by the others — emigrated to open the Spadina restaurant. Since then, three more restaurants have opened. Hong Kong investors have pumped a total of $13 million into them, allowing thirty families to enter the country under the federal government's leaky Business Immigration Program.

There's an aura of mystery — even danger — to Hsin Kuang's Spadina Avenue flagship restaurant. Inside, on the main floor, a group of youths wearing black-leather biker jackets and sullenly chewing toothpicks sprawl around a large table. Two floors up, standing outside one of the many banquet rooms, you can hear the click-click of Mah-Jongg: a group of youths and their girlfriends lean over a board and move the small, ivory cubes as the game requires. When a stranger knocks at the door and asks for permission to watch, she is brusquely ordered downstairs. Below, the manager's assistant ominously warns against bothering the youthful gamblers. "If you stand behind a player, he might think you are bad luck."

Perhaps the most enterprising Chinese restaurateur in Toronto is Eliza Kuok, who is the sister of Lucina Ho, Stanley's wife. Kuok, a thirty-nine-year-old who wears no makeup and has long, coarse dark hair, first came to Canada in August, 1986, with her husband Agostinho, and applied to open a garment factory in Montreal under the Canadian entrepreneur immigration program. When that proposal fell through, the Kuoks invested $225,000 with Peggy and Howard Chan, who run KHK Fashion Group Inc., one of the larger and more successful textile companies in Toronto, which allowed them to obtain conditional visas as investor immigrants. Since her husband's death in a car accident in 1987, Eliza has blossomed as a canny entrepreneur in her own right, opening three new restaurants with lightning speed, including Toronto's most upscale Chinese venue, the Sizzling Pan Chinese Restaurant.

Lucina Ho lent a helping hand by buying the building that houses the restaurant and renting it to her sister. The small, six-table dining room and upstairs banquet room are decorated in subdued greys and dark greens, and have small, Chinese prints on the wall in a style that is suggestive more of English colonial Hong Kong than of traditional Chinese. The ramrod-straight waiters wear white tuxedo shirts, green cummerbunds and green bow ties and pants. Despite her success, Kuok admits over a cup of Chinese tea in the Sizzling Pan that she is not sure whether Canada is good for her. "I had a good business in Hong Kong. I am not afraid of the communists. And it was hard for me to move from one country to another. I feel that since my husband passed away, everything is spoiled here in Canada."

Chinese immigration is bringing new life to the Toronto garment industry, where established Hong Kong–born fashion designers like Alfred Sung are already among the best-known in the country. Small, 2,000- to 10,000-square foot garment shops are opening up in droves along Spadina Avenue and in the industrial area around the Riverdale Chinatown. This fast-growing industry prefers to be anonymous. Many of the factories are hole-in-the-wall affairs, housed in lofts and warehouses, where Chinese workers toil long hours for low wages. "The Chinese workers generally do not join the unions," says Chak-lim Raymond Cheng, owner of Central Garments, a Riverdale textile outfit, and one of Toronto's largest garment factories. "They do not want to make trouble with the employers and they like to work hard."

One of the cheapest places to buy a good leather jacket in Toronto is Imperial Fashions Co. Ltd. in the Spadina garment district. The leather-goods manufacturing company and retail outlet is housed on the first floor and in the basement of a tiny, twelve-foot-wide Victorian semidetached house just off Spadina Avenue. In 1987 two Hong Kong brothers bought it for $130,000, and added $70,000 of capital improvements thereby securing immigration into Canada for themselves and their families. The Tang brothers — Wai Yin and Sun Yin — are hungry-looking men in their forties, their skin stretched tight over high cheekbones. Their father owned and operated a large garment factory in Hong Kong for more than thirty years. Until 1980 it was profitable, producing underwear and cotton T-shirts, and employing about a hundred workers. But, after wage increases in the 1980s squeezed profit margins, the family decided to sell. When the news came that Hong Kong would change hands in 1997, they decided it was time to leave. "We do not like the communists," says Wai Yin. "My father was originally a landowner in mainland China. After the communists came, he fled. Many of our relatives were killed by the communists. I was five or six years old then."

Customers entering the Imperial Fashions building find themselves in a cramped and utilitarian room. There is a sewing machine in the back, and, in the basement, five more sewing machines and a cutting table are squeezed in around the furnace and pipes. Cardboard patterns hang from the basement ceiling and the floor is a chilly, concrete slab. Next to the sewing machines a slow cooker prepares dinner. Even though it is 3:30 in the afternoon, there is no one working in the dank room. "It is hard to find the skillful workers here," says Wai Yin. "I have one male and one female worker. But neither of them came in today." Wai Yin's sullen wife, who sits at the sewing machine on the showroom floor, is tailoring a leather jacket for a customer. Wai Yin, who travels back to Hong Kong each year to oversee some of the work at a sister factory, not owned by the family, in China, is a gentle and obliging retailer. As two young women try on jackets for half an hour, he offers no sales pitch and no slick answers. Indeed, he acts more like an obliging servant, silently fetching the jackets they request and smiling when they are criticized. Eventually, one sister sells herself a jacket; the other walks out of the store empty-handed.

The new breed of Hong Kong entrepreneur is willing to try anything. One of the best examples: James Ting, thirty-eight, the hard-driving, Shanghai-born, Canadian-educated president of a suburban Toronto high-tech company called International Semi-Tech Microelectronics Inc. As noted earlier, in 1987, the Markham, Ontario, outfit was a tiny designer and manufacturer of personal computers whose revenues had never exceeded $27 million in a single year. A year later, it was battling to complete its fourth major acquisition in just eleven months — a $264-million buyout of Shelton, Connecticut–based SSMC Inc., the maker of the famous Singer sewing machines. As the front man for Stanley Ho, Ting has impressive backing. And, Ting's role models are huge, diversified Asian conglomerates, such as Japan's Mitsubishi Corp., in which manufacturing, resources, trading, banking and insurance companies support one another's activities under the same corporate roof.

Ting is by no means alone. The newcomers are willing to try yacht-building, horse-breeding, farms, distilleries — even day care centres. The variety of their enterprises is endless. Patrick Hung, thirty-nine, runs three plastics and electronics manufacturing businesses in Hong Kong, one in China and three in Weston, Ontario, from his new home base in Toronto. After moving to Canada in 1983, he lost money every year for five years. He broke into the black finally in 1988, with clients such as Irwin Toy Ltd. and computer companies who are interested in his new plastic carrying case for personal computer circuit boards. Another entrepreneur, David Chu, produces Ching Chun Bao, the juice-based ginseng drink that is now the rage in Toronto health-food circles and in the Chinese community. Lap Lee employed more than 6,000 workers in China and 1,500 more in Hong Kong. He opened a company, Magnetic Electronics Inc., in the Toronto suburb of Scarborough that manufactures telephone systems for American Telephone & Telegraph Co. Kim Lan Loretta Yip, member of the Hong Kong family that owns Golden Harvest Studios, the second largest film production company in Hong Kong, spent $500,000 to open the Golden Harvest Theatre on Spadina Avenue.

Hong Kong entrepreneurs are so open to new ideas that lawyers and consultants from Toronto make regular pilgrimages to the colony, their briefcases stuffed full of proposals for businesses that are either up for sale or seeking new investment capital. Among the best organized is Toronto lawyer Avi Wisebrod, who assembled a portfolio of 200 businesses for Chinese buyers, which he peddles at the trade fairs that are a staple of the Hong Kong business world. They range from a firm that makes state-of-the-art window-washing equipment to another that produces hydroponic lettuce.

Even Wisebrod admits that the big money from Hong Kong has been channeled mainly into Toronto real estate. That's not too surprising: after all, land is so scarce in Hong Kong that investors traditionally prefer property to just about anything else. More than a third of publicly traded companies listed on the Hong Kong Stock Exchange are involved in real estate development in some way. Even the staggering escalation in Toronto's property prices in recent years hasn't discouraged Hong Kong investors from buying up what, in their eyes, is still cheaply priced real estate.

At one point, in 1987, Hong Kong investors were snapping up houses and condominiums at such a staggering rate that the Real Estate Institute of Canada and the Asia Pacific Business Institute sponsored a one-day crash course at the Royal York Hotel on selling residential property to Hong Kong buyers. Shopping malls are also popular among the newcomers. Since 1986, increasing amounts of Hong Kong money have been moving into active real estate developments throughout the city. Projects looking for Chinese investors fill the classified pages of the Toronto edition of the *Sing Tao* newspaper, which is typeset in Hong Kong and transmitted to Canada each morning by satellite.

But the Hong Kong presence is probably strongest in Toronto's overheated condominium market, where big Canadian condominium developers keep long lists of Hong Kong investors to whom they give priority when a new development begins. Some of the buyers are simply speculators seeking a quick return, who snatch up pre-sale condominiums by making a small down payment and then flip them as soon as the building is ready for occupancy. Others are absentee landlords, who either buy condos for relatives to live in when they immigrate and are laying the groundwork for the family's future in Canada, or simply rent out the properties to Torontonians. Around the city, condos sit empty because the owners, who have an eye on a longer-term investment, are worried that they will become run down if they are rented out.

Whether it is because they grew up on an island, or simply for business reasons, the condo address of choice among Hong Kong investors is the Toronto waterfront, followed by the downtown and Agincourt Chinatowns. Even agencies of the Chinese government are getting in on the action. One Chinese agency has invested in a hotel-and-office condominium complex in Toronto's downtown Chinatown, and is also an investor in a $200-million hotel and office condominium project beside the Scarborough Town Centre.

The biggest Hong Kong players in Toronto real estate are also the biggest players back in their homeland. For proof, you need look no farther than the Harbour Castle Westin which towers over Toronto's overcrowded harbourfront. Contrary to what the name suggests, the Westin Hilton hotel chain does not own the property. Since 1981, Copthorne Holdings Ltd., a company controlled by Li Ka-shing, has held the deed to the property.

Cheng Yu-tung and his partners have earmarked nearly $300 million for a 1,500-unit subdivision in the Toronto bedroom community of Brampton. Through a numbered company, he has also spent $10 million to assemble a block of properties at the corners of University Avenue and Dundas Street where he is building a commercial and office complex. Speculation is that this could be the beginning of an attempt to control the four

corners at University and Dundas and pull the heart of downtown Chinatown eastward.

Cheng's assault on the city is downright tame compared to
that of the Lo family of Hong Kong, which has been snatching
up Toronto hotels at a startling pace since the spring of 1988. If
the three brothers — Lo Ka-shui, Lo Yuk Sui and Vincent —
were better friends, their combined property, construction and
hotel empire would be equivalent to the twentieth-largest company in Hong Kong. Sibling rivalry, though, has prevented a
move toward economies of scale. Instead, the heirs of trader Lo
Ying-shek's thirty-four-year-old property development business have engaged in a sometimes tempestuous four-year effort
to best one another. The disagreements date back to 1984 when
Yuk Sui (Y.S.) teamed up with Australian corporate raider Bill
Wyllie to take on family patriarch Ying-shek and elder brother,
Ka-shui, to wrest control of the family's troubled hotel holdings.
After a complex series of share swaps and controversial fund-
raising moves, Y.S. ended up with a controlling share in the
family's real estate investment firm, Paliburg Investments, and a
troubled Kowloon hotel.

Since then, Y.S. has used his genius for corporate finance to
build a majority stake in a number of publicly listed companies
in Hong Kong and North America, and to swing a number of
astute and profitable real estate deals. Perhaps even more impressive is the fact that, within just five years, he has built a single
ailing hotel into the upscale Regal hotel chain, the world's
twentieth-largest hospitality chain.

In June, 1988, Y.S. paid an estimated $58 million for a control-
ling interest in the 900-room Constellation Hotel, which is
located near Toronto's Pearson International Airport. This
wasn't a spur-of-the-moment decision. Lo searched for two
years and considered twenty other Canadian hotels before
choosing the Constellation. But when he decided to move he
did so in typically aggressive Hong Kong fashion. "He walked in
here dressed in a sweater and trench coat and said I am going to

give you x amount for your hotel," recalls George Kalmar, who had been the sole owner of the Constellation since 1972. "The deal took fifteen minutes." The hotel now displays a large brass "Regal Constellation" sign on its facade. Lo's goal is to draw in more international business travelers, particularly the many from Hong Kong and the Pacific Rim who are familiar with the Regal name.

Y.S.'s younger brother Vincent has also shown a taste for corporate razzle-dazzle, and a willingness, indeed, even desire, to take on Y.S. whenever the opportunity arises. The two, who have reportedly not spoken to each other since the 1984 struggle, faced off in bids (both unsuccessful) for the Vancouver Meridien Hotel in September, 1988. Now the Toronto real estate market is the feuding brothers' newest battleground.

Only three months after Y.S.'s move on the Constellation, Shui On Group, chaired by Vincent, bought the 388-room Wharton Renaissance Hotel and the 300-room Ramada Hotel–Airport West for $83 million. Vincent created Shui On Group in 1971 with $100,000 and a loan from his father. Since going public in 1983, Shui On has become one of Hong Kong's thirty largest companies, with operations that range from property development to trading with mainland China. A subsidiary of Shui On explores opportunities in the hotel, entertainment and leisure businesses. Vincent's eclectic and forward-looking management style has become legendary in Hong Kong. Unlike the more autocratic, family-based Hong Kong entrepreneurs, he is open to suggestion and regularly meets with senior management executives to discuss ways to improve business and productivity. Employees are compensated under an elaborate system known as the Hay System by which they are awarded points for each job based on its level of difficulty and responsibility.

Not all the Hong Kong money is brand-new. The Wong family of Hong Kong, another major player in Toronto real estate, has had a presence here since 1974, when they paid $5.2 million to buy LuCliff Place, a twenty-four-story office, commercial and apartment tower on Bay Street, at the eastern periphery of Toronto's downtown Chinatown. Clifford Wong, the patriarch of the clan, was an architecture graduate of Montreal's McGill University in 1960. He left soon after graduation, to build a thriving family business in Hong Kong. Wong, who gave $1 million to his McGill alma mater in 1986, died a year later. His daughter Mary-Jean, who graduated from the University of Toronto and married a Toronto physician, ran the Canadian end of the business until she returned to Hong Kong in 1988, to work on the firm's 6,000-house residential subdivision in the New Territories. Now Wong's son-in-law, Nelson Chen, holds the reins on the Canadian side of the family operations and entertains proposals for real estate investments or projects.

Another quiet — but powerful — Hong Kong presence in Toronto real estate is C.W. Yeung. He made his money in the 1960s, by buying up property at Depression-like prices when the Chinese Red Guard marched into Hong Kong and the wealthiest families were selling for whatever they could fetch. Today, Yeung, who is best known in Hong Kong as the owner of King Fok Jewelers, owns eight downtown Toronto commercial properties which are worth about $200 million. But he started small in Toronto. A key purchase occurred in 1975, when Yeung and his Toronto agent paid $1 million for a Mr Submarine franchise on the busy downtown corner of Yonge and Adelaide streets. As developers attempted to assemble the block, the property soared in value, and in 1979 they auctioned it off for $3 million. A year later, they paid $20 million for a posh Yonge Street commercial property which his partner, a young and aggressive Chinese man, was hot to flip for a quick profit ten months later. Yeung insisted on holding on. It paid off: today the property is worth $60-70 million. "He is the most impassive investor," says one observer."He just wants to get money out of Hong Kong. He owns acres of property in California, Hawaii and New York. And he won't sell."

Others are building their reputations, and fortunes, here in Canada. Henry Hung, who is best known as the developer of

the Dragon City Mall, is a prime example. Hung's company,
Shiu Pong Enterprises, is housed in a renovated warehouse off
of Spadina Avenue. Like advertisements of wealth, an Audi and
a BMW are parked on boulevard pads in front of the in-
conspicuous building. In the company's waiting room, a large,
velvety-black fish, which Hung explains is there to absorb any
bad luck coming in the door, swims in a tank of water. Dressed
casually in a white shirt, cardigan and flashy tie, Henry Hung
seems almost boyish as he explains how he built a net worth of
$10 million virtually from scratch — all before the age of thirty-
seven. After earning an economics degree from the University
of Toronto and an MBA from the University of Windsor, he
invested passively in Toronto real estate until 1980, when he
started to do small-scale renovation projects in Toronto's An-
nex area. Three years later he began developing properties full
time. He used money from his parents in Hong Kong to buy the
land and then obtained financing for development from local
banks. The move into the big time came in 1984 when Hung,
using $2 million from his parents, bought a roller-skating rink in
Scarborough, spent $1 million on renovations and created an
indoor mall with a Chinese theme, which he called the Dragon
Centre. "Most people would have said, why don't we just do a
better skating rink? Especially because the building is not on a
main artery. But I could see the potential." The masterstroke
came two years later, however, when he and Daniel managed to
buy the site of a Hungarian Catholic church on the corner of
Dundas and Spadina where the Dragon City Mall now stands.
"Chinatown has nowhere else to go but up and down Spadina,"
he says matter-of-factly. "We knew it was going to be an important corner." Even so, luck can change. As the authors left
Hung's office following the interview, they wondered about the
significance of the talisman black fish now lying motionless at
the bottom of the tank. Perhaps it was only sleeping.

Some of the new Chinese Canadians are getting rich by
selling real estate rather than buying it; people like Frank Chau,

president of Goldyear Realty Inc., and Chinatown's best-known realtor. Born into a wealthy Hong Kong family in 1946, Chau is a tall, self-possessed businessman who walks through Chinatown with the confident air of someone who knows its secrets. When Chau, his property manager, Tak Chen and Francis Kwong, who invests money for his Hong Kong–based family, enter the Chinatown International Chinese Restaurant, diners at four or five tables turn to greet them. Joining them for lunch is another wealthy Hong Kong immigrant who is effusive in his praise of Chau's business skills. "You are very efficient," he says warmly. "You can talk the birds down from the trees."

Chau specializes in commercial real estate, particularly in setting up private, syndicated real estate deals for investors. Using a network of Canadian and Hong Kong investors, he buys up bargain-priced commercial buildings and office towers when the original developers have gone bankrupt, or acquires new shopping centres that the owners are having difficulty leasing.

During a meal that consisted of barbecued ribs, pork, squid, giant clams, egg custards, congee (a kind of rice soup), duck and Tsingtao beer, Chau describes one of his greatest coups. Acting for a group of wealthy Hong Kong investors, he paid $14 million to buy a five-acre shopping centre in Mississauga after the original developers were unable to attract tenants. The new owners hope that the development, called the Mississauga Chinese Centre, will be the beginning of Toronto's fifth Chinatown. Its design fuses a modern shopping centre with life-size or nearly life-size reproductions of major Chinese land-marks. A scaled-down Great Wall separates the plaza and its parking lot. The colonnade is a recreation of one found in China's Summer Palace Garden. And, pagoda-style roofs made of green ceramic tiles decorate the entrance to the development. "I have been in business long enough that every time we have a project, we can sell it within our own group of contacts," Chau says between sips of tea. Indeed, later, while driving his grey

Mercedes 420 SEL to Mississauga, he dials Hawaii on his ever-present cellular phone to talk to one of them.

In Hong Kong, the big Chinese guns like Stanley Ho, Cheng Yu-tung and Li Ka-shing are used to chipping in together on investments; if Li is in on something good, he will cut in Ho, and vice versa. It is not as though they could not cover most investments themselves; it is more a matter of respect and a gesture promising cooperation in the future. The same spirit has been carried into Canada. A good example is the Brampton subdivision jointly developed by Cheng Yu-tung and Lee Shau-kee. At the same time, the same two businessmen have competed fiercely against each other for downtown Toronto properties. Both, for instance, put in competing bids for the choice property immediately to the east of Li Ka-shing's Harbour Castle Westin. Cheng's bid was the highest at $42 million, but the city's Harbour Commission decided against either bid and sold it for just $25 million to competing buyers from the Toronto suburb of North York.

Hong Kong developers behave far differently than their Canadian counterparts. As one Toronto city planning department official explains it: "In Hong Kong if you want more density, you can pay for it. Their system works with payoffs. Our process is more democratic and complex, and a lot of Hong Kong people would simply prefer not to be exposed to it. In Toronto, we have a media that scrutinizes development and Hong Kong investors are terrified of it. When confronted, they back away and do what the zoning says they are supposed to do. It is a big step for them to apply for re-zoning."

The Hong Kong bias toward modern architectural design has proven even more controversial. "There are a whole myriad of Chinese architects running around with preconceived ideas of what they want to see, and it may have no relevance or bearing to the structures around them," says one established Toronto architect who wants to remain nameless. Adds another: "The Hong Kong Chinese simply have no sensitivity to the historical evolution of Toronto. In their eyes, everything old is ugly and they describe the city's Victorian buildings as 'low class.' For people from Hong Kong, everything has to be big and shiny and new."

Michael Wong, the architect of choice for the big Hong Kong investors coming to Canada, has to shoulder some of this criticism. The exodus of big money out of Hong Kong is the best thing that has happened to him since the U.S. oil boom of the late 1970s. Back then, Wong was selling most of his designs in places like Denver, Oklahoma and Dallas. Today, the forty-nine-year-old architect with the bowl-shaped haircut derives nearly half his income from Hong Kong clients. In his austere offices in the Eaton Centre's north tower, he designs office towers and commercial projects for a veritable Who's Who of the Hong Kong elite, including people like Cheng Yu-tung and Lee Shau-kee.

But the man who may really be responsible for changing the Toronto skyline is not an architect at all, but a master of *feng-shui* (pronounced "fung soy") the mystical Chinese geomancy of location and design. Invented in China more than 2,000 years ago as a land-surveying technique, *feng-shui* — literally "wind and rain" — holds that a lucky environment depends on balancing the elements of water, earth, fire, wood and metal. To Western ears, this may sound like mumbo jumbo, but in Hong Kong the influence of *feng-shui* is everywhere. Hong Kong's colonial government has long compensated rural villagers whose *feng-shui* has been disrupted by land development, and whole villages have sometimes been abandoned because the local *feng-shui* has been disturbed. European miners even had to be imported to build the colony's first railway tunnels because Chinese workers refused to disturb the earth spirits.

Today, even the wealthiest Hong Kong developer would not consider constructing a new building without asking a *feng-shui* master how it should be designed and what materials to use. The reason: merchants believe business failures occur when the natural, harmonious movement of spirits is thrown into confusion by misplaced pillars, tables, windows or television antennas. Buildings must be properly positioned on the street. Their doors, windows, furniture, plants and vases must be painstakingly placed to maximize luck. Even if they don't believe it themselves, developers and real estate agents who ignore *feng-shui* run the risk of alienating the scores of wealthy Chinese who do. That is why the developer of the ultramodern, $650-million Hong Kong & Shanghai Bank building slated for Hong Kong prudently had its blueprints vetted by *feng-shui* experts, and followed the masters' advice to move a bank officer's door away from a nearby escalator to preserve the delicate yin-yang. In Singapore, which is 76 per cent Chinese, the Hyatt Regency hotel was suffering from a lack of business in 1971 when a *feng-shui* master advised that the hotel's fountain and facade be remodeled to rid the hotel of unhappy spirits and lure back Chinese guests discouraged by stories of its bad *feng-shui*. Management acted on the advice and, today, the hotel is thriving.

In Toronto, Hong Kong entrepreneurs who are worried about angering the spirits flock to Ivan Yip, who has been dabbling in *feng-shui* and astrology for more than thirty years. He is a slightly built fifty-three-year-old with thick glasses. Recently retired from his job as a forensic scientist with the Ontario government, Yip now spends his days dispensing advice on how to position and build new developments and how to pick existing homes without disrupting the cosmic forces. Anyone who wants to see Yip has to wait two weeks for an appointment. And he does not come cheap: he might charge $25,000 to analyse a $10-million development, while smaller projects cost $100 an hour. That is still low compared to the $185,000 which the Hong Kong & Shanghai Bank paid a *feng-shui* master to prepare his study of the billion-dollar glass and steel tower in Hong Kong.

Yip has already worked on many of the major Chinese projects in Metro Toronto, including the 10,000-square-foot Hsin Kuang restaurant in Mississauga and the 11,000-square foot Oriental Ocean restaurant opened in Scarborough. He helps real estate companies pick lucky houses for Hong Kong buyers. He even has non-Chinese clients, like the real estate arm of a life insurance company, which commissioned him to prepare a lengthy *feng-shui* study of a planned $300-million international banking centre for downtown Toronto. When the project's architects presented him with sketches of two triangular towers — which were unstable according to the teachings of *feng-shui* — Yip recommended a major re-design. He urged the developers to change the traffic flow into and out of the parking garage so that the cars could not drive straight through to the next street. According to *feng-shui* thought, that meant that money could flow straight through the building without stopping. Yip also drew up plans showing how the building should be positioned to take advantage of the flow of power and money from the Parliament Buildings in Ottawa, Toronto's nearby City Hall and New York City's Wall Street district.

Sitting before a jumble of papers in the kitchen of his Toronto home, Yip shakes his head when asked if *feng-shui* has anything to do with magic. It is a matter of harmony, he says. One of Yip's *feng-shui* theories holds that human beings have iron in their blood which responds to the earth's magnetic field. "Suppose your iron content is compatible with the magnetic field. If you spend at least one-third of your time well-positioned in that field, your mind will be crystal clear, and you can make the right decisions." Where a person is living is so important to the calculation of luck that Yip says a person can be lucky in Toronto but not in Hong Kong. And, accordingly, luck can change dramatically from one year to the next.

His rules for buying real estate without disturbing the cosmic forces are endless. Houses facing a T-intersection or cul-de-sac, or overlooking a funeral home or graveyard, are thought to bring bad luck. So are buildings that face the edge of another building, since the edge constitutes a threatening sharp object. Lampposts or big trees in front of the door block the flow of luck. Houses with front doors directly at the foot of the main staircase, or which open to allow a view directly to the back of the house, are thought to be unlucky. It is also considered unwise to buy a building, or build beside, a high tower, since that is tantamount to building under the slope of a mountain. Rectangular buildings are the best to buy, but square buildings are okay, too. Condo units bearing the numbers two, three and eight go the fastest because those numbers bring luck and prosperity. If all three numbers are combined, they consider it the best possible combination for success. Indeed, licence plates throughout Hong Kong bear these numbers. At the same time, condo units with the number four in their address sell poorly to Hong Kong buyers. The reason: four sounds remarkably like the Chinese word for death.

Anyone who does business with Chinese developers ignores *feng-shui* at his peril. Toronto lawyer Mendel Green specializes in helping foreign investors, particularly those from Hong Kong, invest in Canada. He may, or may not be a believer in the dicta of *feng-shui*, but he has even gone to the trouble to decorate his office in accordance with *feng-shui* principles. This probably makes him the only Jewish lawyer in the country in whose office you will see a geomancer's compass and a four-dimensional Buddha correctly positioned to face the door. Green even took the somewhat extreme step of moving a door facing an associate's office because, in *feng-shui*, opposing doors can cause a personality confrontation between the occupants of the two offices. "At one point, we were going to move out of this building," says Green. "But I decided the *feng-shui* was good for us here."

Going to these sorts of lengths would not be necessary but for one inescapable fact: Hong Kong investors have become some of the biggest players in Toronto real estate. How big? Some observers, like Harvey Kaufman, director of sales for Norman

Hill & Associates Ltd., a Toronto real estate company, say that the influx of Chinese money is the single biggest factor driving the city's real estate market which has been roaring out of control since 1986. That view, however, is far from being unanimously held. Indeed, Rashmi Nathwani, the City Property Commissioner for Toronto, thinks Hong Kong investors account for only 5 to 10 per cent of the real estate investment in the city. In his view, Canadian pension funds are a far greater force on the upward trend in prices. Avi Wisebrod, who often acts for Hong Kong buyers, says blaming his clients for Toronto's overheated housing prices is totally absurd. "There are 40,000 immigrants coming to Toronto annually, coming from everywhere from Regina to Hong Kong. Why are we surprised that prices are going up and why are we so sure that the Chinese are behind it?"

In fact, anyone who has ever watched Chinese investors conduct business would know that they likely have little to do with Toronto's skyrocketing real estate prices. When it comes to negotiating, the Chinese are discriminating buyers who seldom pay up for properties. And when they take a position, that is that. "You can dance from here until next Thursday and they will not budge," says Avi Wisebrod. One Canadian observer watchd Chinese executives working for Cheng Yu-tung negotiate with a flock of senior vice-presidents from a major Canadian oil company over a property which Cheng wanted. After Cheng's aides made their offer, the oilmen excused themselves from the room and returned minutes later with a counter proposal. The response of Cheng's negotiator: "I have explained what we will do and why." Again they left the room and returned with another proposal. Again the Chinese repeated their unwavering position. For two hours the process was repeated. Finally, the oilmen decided that arguing further was useless. Cheng's quiet patience won him the deal he wanted.

Their knowledge about the Toronto real estate market is startling. They do their homework, and depend upon a wide network of friends, relatives and agents in Toronto with whom they can cross-check property values. Wisebrod recalls that he once mentioned to William Doo, one of his clients, that a particular Toronto hotel was up for sale. Before Wisebrod could offer more information, Doo rhymed off the details of several existing offers on the building and the reasons why no deal had yet been concluded. Recalls Wisebrod: "It was impressive. When a Hong Kong investor gives you chapter, line and verse on a property on your home turf it can be pretty embarrassing."

Mendel Green knows all about the business acumen of the newcomers from Hong Kong. Normally he runs a computer software program to analyse the cash flow of buildings and the prices of real estate in a particular area. But Hong Kong buyers rarely accept his analysis of property values. They prefer to depend upon their own experience and range of contracts. "But, you have to remember that there is a substantial difference in psyche between the Hong Kong and Canadian real estate investor," says Green over a cup of Chinese tea at his law office, in the midst of Toronto's downtown financial district. "They are not investing their life's future in Canada. What they invest here represents only a small portion of their net worth. They are securing the future of their immediate family and future generations".

Green, like so many other experts, thinks North American investors can learn a lot from Hong Kong's hard-working cap-italists and shrewd investors. He remembers shaking his head in disbelief at one Hong Kong client who was considering buying a building which would have cost him $150,000 a year just in financing costs. The client went ahead with the deal, despite Green's objections, and told the lawyer that he did not under-stand his motives. A week after the deal was closed, a local land assembler offered to buy the property at a price which gave Green's client a tidy $1-million profit. "The key to the Asians' success in North America is that they are not as short-sighted as we are," concludes the Toronto lawyer.

His point is well taken. After all, the rich refugees from Hong Kong are certainly altering the city's skyline and the mix of its neighborhoods, and even transforming staid Toronto society in the process. But, their most lasting impact may well be in reshaping the way business is conducted in Canada's financial and business centre. The irresistible dynamism of Hong Kong commerce is already making its presence felt in Toronto. And, for the city's complacent businessmen and financiers, the challenge may well be either to learn to swim with the Hong Kong tide — or be swept under by it.

6/ VANCOUVER: A CITY DIVIDED

The air in the packed hall was thick with the heat of anger and resentment. Under normal circumstances, the auditorium at the Kerrisdale Seniors Centre has room to seat 260, but these were not normal circumstances. On the afternoon of Sunday, February 26, 1989, nearly 700 people, many of them white-haired, frail senior citizens, were crammed into the spare Vancouver community hall. The meeting had been called by a local senior citizens' group. They were bewildered and worried. A large number of apartments and landmark Tudor-style cottages in their comfortable, upper-middle-class neighborhood had recently been sold and then demolished to make room for more profitable, and exceedingly more expensive, rental and condominium high-rises. The elderly residents wanted answers from the seven aldermen and ten provincial politicians who were seated, uncomfortably, on the stage in the front of the room. But it quickly became apparent that the crowd was also there to vent its rage at the Asian immigrants who had been pouring into the neighborhood, and who, they suspected, were behind the transformation of their beloved Kerrisdale.

Outside the hall hovered a knot of noisy younger men and women. They were wearing white T-shirts emblazoned with the word "Hongcouver." Inside the tone was nastier. Several people tried to tack up crude anti-foreigner and anti–Hong Kong signs on the walls, and had to be ejected by the organizers. Drawing their worn coats over their delicate shoulders, the elderly crowd booed and hissed the politicians and struggled to hear as one older man shouted that the price of Vancouver land was being set in Hong Kong. Another long-time local demanded that the government prevent non-residents from buying residential property in British Columbia. Cried one woman in her thirties, one of the youngsters in the audience: "When are you going to start changing things?"

The scene was chaotic and unsettling, and a telling indication of the way in which Vancouver — the laid-back, hedonistic Malibu of the North — is being turned inside-out by the dramatic influx of Asian wealth. Once merely a vague rumor, Hong Kong money is now the piston that drives Vancouver as, each year, $1 to 2 billion of investment and 5,000 new immigrants flee the British Colony for the mountain-locked, sea-washed Canadian city of 1.4 million. As a result, there has been a palpable change in attitude in the once-small sawmill town at the end of the Canadian Pacific Railway. Bordered by the Rocky Mountains to the east and the Pacific Ocean to the west, Vancouver has always hovered in the Canadian psyche as much a state of mind as an actual place, a refuge for burned-out Easterners who have hung up their briefcases to sunbathe nude on Wreck Beach, windsurf off Jericho Beach and hotdog on Grouse Mountain. Armed with a fierce business savvy forged in the world's most competitive market, Hong Kong's capitalists are reshaping Vancouver in the image of Pacific Rim metropolises like San Francisco, Los Angeles, Singapore and Tokyo. No city in the world, in fact, has been so changed by Hong Kong money

as has Vancouver. And residents of Kerrisdale, like other Vancouverites, are learning that what Hong Kong money wants, it
usually gets.

There are signs of prosperity wherever you look in the once-
sleepy streets. Take a stroll through the thriving downtown
business core, where nearly all the construction going on in the
spring of 1989 was fueled by Hong Kong money. Flip at random
through the pages of the *Sun* or *Province*, Vancouver's two
daily newspapers, and glance at the pages of advertisements for
homes and condominiums which cost, on average, 25 per cent
more than just a year ago. Drive through Kerrisdale, which has
become the city's newest Chinese enclave, and look up into the
second-floor window at the corner house which has just been
sold for $1.4 million, where a young Chinese girl sits studiously
writing at a desk. Walk down the street, where Chinese pre-
schoolers play on the front lawns of two new large brick houses
squeezed in between traditional Vancouver Tudors. Wander
through the city's bustling fourteen-block Chinatown on the
eastern end of the downtown peninsula, where even a run-
down, insect-ridden storefront building now fetches $1.5 to $2
million, as new Hong Kong families push the community's
borders farther and farther out. Pay a visit to the Main Street
Chinatown branch of the HongKong Bank of Canada, the
fastest-growing of all of the bank's fifty-eight Canadian
branches. Have a chat with David Lee, the forty-eight-year-old
manager, who has watched his branch's loans swell from $3
million to $100 million in just two and a half years, and who
predicts that its loan portfolio will climb to $200 million within
the next two years, virtually all of it offshore Asian money.

Vancouverites, it is safe to say, saw their future in December,
1987, when B.C. premier Bill Vander Zalm announced that the
former site of Expo 86 — literally one-sixth of Vancouver's
downtown — had been awarded to Concord Pacific Developments Ltd., a company controlled by Li Ka-shing, together with
Cheng Yu-tung and Lee Shau-kee. Li's $2-billion plan to turn

the one-time rail yard, on the north shore of Vancouver's picturesque False Creek, into a high-density mixture of office towers, commercial space and housing, stands to be the largest real estate deal in Vancouver since 1884, when the Canadian Pacific Railway was granted most of the present-day city by the provincial government. Once complete, this "mini–Hong Kong," without a doubt, will change the face of the city. Yet, Li, Lee and Cheng are only the crest of the Asian wave washing over Vancouver.

The Chinese community has been part of the local fabric since the late nineteenth century. But the downtrodden miners, railway laborers, cooks and laundrymen who made their way in the inhospitable new land more than a century ago bear little resemblance to the educated, wealthy newcomers who have become the architects of the city's future. Of the 22,802 Hong Kong immigrants who headed for Canada in 1988, 4,817 chose Vancouver. Overall, that means only 20 per cent of Vancouver's new residents came from the British colony. But if the numbers don't impress, the wealth behind them do. Many of the newcomers were members of Hong Kong's richest families. The end result is that Vancouver, with its 150,000 Chinese residents, likely has more Hong Kong dollars per capita than anywhere else in the country. Says Michael Goldberg, a University of British Columbia professor who has written a book on Chinese investment and now heads the province's International Financial Centre: "Toronto gets the professional, managerial Hong Kong immigrants. Vancouver gets the yacht people."

People like Hong Kong lawyer Sydney Leong, the secretive chairman of AGIFEL Properties, whose Canadian assets are thought to approach $500 million. In 1984 he paid an estimated $85 million for Lansdowne Park Shopping Centre in suburban Richmond. While he remains in Hong Kong, his five children live in Canada. Lincoln and Winston, his two eldest boys, make their homes in Vancouver and run the Canadian operations.

Stanley Ho, the fox-trotting gambling magnate of Macao, owns the downtown Le Meridien Hotel, as well as some other attractive Vancouver turf. Then there's Sally Au Sian, another absentee landlord, who controls the Sing Tao Group, a $150-million publishing, property and pharmaceuticals conglomerate. In Canada her companies own Chinese-language newspapers in Vancouver and Toronto, office and apartment blocks in both cities, and a shopping plaza in Richmond, B.C.

There are also Peter Eng, K.K. Wong and Edward Woo, who are partners in Allied Holdings Ltd., which developed a downtown condominium complex called Albernia Place. They also own shopping centres, a hotel and an entire city block near Vancouver's Hastings Street.

And, that's just for starters. The Who's Who list also includes Patrick Tse, who is probably better known in Hong Kong where he was a major film star, than in Vancouver where he and his wife, Deborah, run one of the city's budding garment companies. Also on the list is Thomas Fung, the son of the founder of Hong Kong's powerful Sun Hung Kai Securities. He lives in Vancouver and owns a company called Fairchild Developments Ltd., as well as a trendy Chinese bakery called St. Germain Bakery. The circle, as well, includes Au Bak Ling, an extremely low-profile Hong Kong investor who still lives in the British colony, but is building a $19-million Vancouver condo development. Let's not forget about Danny Gaw, who is known in Vancouver as the west coast's doughnut king because his Max's Donuts Ltd. doughnut chain turns out 84,000 doughnuts a day. The list goes on and on and on.

Naturally, real estate is where the lion's share of the Hong Kong money is going — naturally, because most of the rich newcomers made their fortunes in property back in their homeland. Besides, given British Columbia's natural resource-based economy, and lack of manufacturing base, what else is there to invest in? The most common approach among Hong Kongers is to buy up houses and condos, sometimes in huge numbers, and then either hold them until after 1997, or move in now. Buses and limousines regularly meet flights from Hong Kong and other Asian cities to take visitors on house- and condo-buying tours. In one legendary case, an Asian buyer toured nineteen West Vancouver homes and bought all but one. Vancouver businessmen still speak in awe about the enterprising fellow, the owner of a chain of taxis in Hong Kong, who went into the property business in Vancouver: he made $12 million in a couple years by building condos. But, for success stories it is hard to beat the retiree who came to Vancouver from Hong Kong two and a half years ago with $3 million in his pocket. A few sharp real estate investments later and he now calculates his net worth in the hundreds of millions.

Hong Kong buyers are snapping up new homes at such a rate that engineer Zenon Scheller estimates that 40 per cent of the new houses under construction in Vancouver are now being built by developers exclusively to attract Hong Kong clients. Many are being sold while still at the blueprint stage. Says Frits Huckride, Scheller's partner: "If you build a house in Kerrisdale, you can be assured of selling it to Hong Kong money." Meanwhile, the Hong Kong appetite for condos, which are the purchase of choice because the upkeep is easy, is so fierce that developers have recently flooded the market with 3,000 to 4,000 new condominium units. So pervasive is their influence that housing officials and developers agree that half the condominium projects in Vancouver would fold if the Hong Kong money took flight. "People want to sell their condos before Li Ka-shing's Expo lands development comes on the market," explains Vancouver realtor Robert MacArthur. "There is a big scare that he can undercut everyone else's condo prices because he paid so little for the land." As for other properties, during 1987 and 1988, twenty major hotels changed hands in greater Vancouver, fifteen going to Asian buyers. The list includes the

New World Harbourside, bought by Cheng Yu-tung, Ho's Meridien, the historic Georgia Hotel, which mainland Chinese interests sold to Caleb Chan, and the Pacific Palisades Hotel which was bought by the Kuok family.

If you really want an idea of the extent of offshore money pouring into Vancouver property, just visit commercial real estate broker Andrea Eng's office at Colliers Macaulay Nicholls Inc., where she keeps a table-size map of Vancouver showing the prime downtown blocks. Eng, who is thirty-three years old, is a former beauty queen and second-generation Canadian from a Chinese family. She uses pastel markers to keep a record of which Asian nationalities own what in downtown Vancouver. "Yellow is for the Hong Kong Chinese," she chirps. "Blue is for the local Chinese and pink is for Singapore."

Eng says that new and old Chinese only own about 7 per cent of downtown. "For them, it is a diversification process," she says, "not a way to escape 1997, and definitely not a bargain." Even so, Eng personally sold nearly $200 million worth of Vancouver real estate last year — almost all to offshore buyers. And, at a glance, the markings seem to cover a generous portion of the map. Ernest Hui's Park Georgia Properties is colored yellow, for Hong Kong Chinese, even though he has lived here since 1968. Another dab of yellow is for Alberni Place. A series of pink blocks in an L-shape stand out on the map. "Oh that's Robert Kuok," says Eng. "A group from Toronto got hold of the Pacific Palisades Hotel — the pink — and immediately flipped it to Kuok for a $2-million profit. He subsequently bought the 1200 and 1300 blocks [the figures refer to street numbers]. I suppose that is to protect his view corridors [to the mountains]. There is also talk that he plans to build a hotel on the 1300-block site. He did all that in 1988. He just came in there and laid down a whole pot of money — probably $60 million."

There is other action in town besides property. Government figures show that Asian immigrants entering Canada under

Ottawa's Business Immigration Program shifted more than $1 billion into the B.C. economy in 1988. Their investments spanned everything from restaurants and garment factories to fish farms and high-technology companies. There is, for example, a Hong Kong yarn-and-thread company which has bought a factory in nearby Port Coquitlam and will spend another $2.5 million upgrading and importing machinery to run a yard-and-thread mill. Or Johnny Cheung, who spent $1 million to open Vincci Watch International Corp., which uses B.C. jade and black onyx, as well as other minerals, to manufacture watches for export. Cheung is not the only one in his family engaged in manufacturing; his brother-in-law's company manufactures plastic shopping bags in Delta, B.C.

This, of course, is small potatoes compared to B.C.'s mammoth forestry, mining and tourism industries. Some experts, such as Michael Goldberg, take the view that Hong Kong investment has been grossly exaggerated and has contributed little to B.C.'s recovery. "Hong Kong investment in B.C. is peanuts," says Goldberg. "We got out of the recession in 1986 with the help of Expo. It was a classic case of Keynesian spending. There were construction expenditures. Then there was a flood of tourists and high pulp and logging prices."

All the same, investment and immigration from Hong Kong, Taiwan and the East represents Vancouver's best opportunity to break its dependence on boom-or-bust resource industries, and to develop faster than its other Pacific-coast rivals, like Seattle and San Francisco. Offshore investment, in fact, is a gift which British Columbia never expected, a shower of gold on a region whose future has always been determined by the vagaries of commodity markets. Notes Michael Walker, chairman of the Fraser Institute, a free enterprise–oriented Vancouver-based think tank: "Wherever the Chinese have gone, whether Singapore, Hong Kong, Indonesia or Malaysia, in spite of being discriminated against, bashed around, miserably treated and not allowed to vote, they invariably perform economic miracles. We should be encouraging them any way we can, rather than talking about the negative factors."

Not everyone shares this optimism. Vancouver is a city divided, eager to cash in on its breathtaking windfall, but worried that its leafy, quiet streets and laid-back life-style could disappear forever. The influx of Asian wealth and the Asian wealthy have touched almost everyone living in the city. The building boom is making developers and construction companies very, very rich. Ditto realtors like Andrea Eng. And, the same goes for the scores of lawyers, accountants and consultants who service the monied newcomers. One Vancouver law firm did $400,000 worth of Asian business in the first two months of 1989 alone. But, more again blame the wealthy immigrants for everything from skyrocketing housing prices, to overcrowded schools and dramatically changing neighborhoods. "I am reminded of that line by Kurt Vonnegut," said one Vancouver advertising executive, referring to the rape of North American Indian land by white settlers. "We are the Indians now."

There is no missing the resentment. Real estate has become the consuming topic of conversation among Vancouverites. Some people argue that the real cause of the housing boom is simple supply and demand. Locked in by mountains, the ocean and rich agricultural reserve land, it is estimated that Vancouver has only 70,000 single-family homes and few vacant lots on which to build new ones. The land shortage, so the logic goes, has pushed housing prices prohibitively high. Even so, young, first-time home buyers and average income earners blame the Asian influence for ensuring that they can no longer afford to live in Vancouver, where the average house price has climbed from $113,000 in 1985 to $200,000 four years later. Indeed, a survey by real estate company Royal LePage shows that in 1988 only 30 per cent of home buyers in Greater Vancouver were first-time purchasers, the lowest level in Canada.

The outcry has also been long and loud over the Asian penchant for razing typical Vancouver homes to make room for what, in the eyes of many Anglo-Vancouverites, are "monster" houses that fill an entire lot. Chinese developers are also being blamed for the elimination of rental housing in Vancouver. The average rents in Vancouver's West End apartment area are seventy to eighty cents a square foot. But new construction requires rent of at least $1.30 to $1.50 a square foot, meaning $2,000 to $3,000 per unit. For that reason, most new high-rise residential buildings have been condominiums instead of rentals, and apartment buildings are being razed to make room for the more lucrative condos. "The developers are not all Chinese — only about half of them are," says Don Vassos, a senior vice-president at Vancouver's Coldwell Banker Canada Inc. "But as far as the public and the press is concerned, it might as well be all of them."

There has been a huge furor over the growing number of new Vancouver condo projects which have been sold to offshore Hong Kong investors before the locals have even had a chance to bid, and then flipped for a quick, usually large, profit. Even Victor Li himself was shocked by the angry response when he sold the Regatta condominiums on the south shore of False Creek to Hong Kong buyers without an offering in Vancouver. "I was not being sensitive enough to local feelings, and I misjudged market response and local demand," Li told reporters.

The overheated Vancouver housing market and the shortage of affordable housing have become hot political issues in Vancouver. The housing question even helped to decide an important provincial by-election in the affluent Point Grey area in March, 1989, during which all three candidates tried to top each other in proposed measures to stop real estate speculation. In a stunning upset, the NDP candidate took the riding, which had been Socred for fourteen years. Analysts blamed the Socred slump in popularity on the fact that B.C. has been without subsidized housing programs since the early 1980s. Meanwhile, Vancouver's city council is now developing amendments to zoning and development bylaws that would guarantee tenants six months to find new accommodation before a developer can demolish their apartment building.

As the debate rages, the tone gets dirtier. The local media, particularly Vancouver's newspapers, refuse to let the Asian question rest. Every morning, the editors find some new angle on the problem, headlining everything from families disenfranchised by Hong Kong money to triads, the Chinese crime gangs which are said to have agents in every overseas Chinese community. The press coverage has so angered the Hong Kong newcomers that several have even discussed buying Pacific Press Ltd., which prints both the *Sun* and the *Province*, to silence the critics.

The city's CBC television station gave viewers an indication of how deep-seated the tensions are when it aired a special nightly segment on Hong Kong investment in B.C. in the spring of 1989. Some unsavory views surfaced when the CBC invited a studio audience to question community leaders about the Hong Kong phenomenon. The low point came when Douglas Collins, a British-born former newspaper reporter and virulent opponent of Asian immigration, stood up and suggested to the mayor that the city should send a message to Hong Kong, saying that it has a new motto: "We surrender." Said Collins: "This has become an Asiatic city." A horrified Andrea Eng, who was part of the panel, gasped: "I am shocked." But Vancouver mayor Gordon Campbell struck an elegant counterblow by asking whether he detected an accent in Collins's voice.

But it will take more than a few words to stop the spreading xenophobia. On street corners, vendors peddling "Hong-couver" T-shirts make a killing. One doctor's wife made known her view about the design of a house under construction in the Kerrisdale area by spray painting "This is an ugly home" on its unfinished side. At dinner parties among the white thirty-something crowd, the "Hong Kong invasion" is a frequent topic of conversation. Joked one executive: "These Chinese guys are scary. Remember at the University of Toronto, they used to study all night on the top floor of the Robarts Library, even on weekends!" Adds Jack Webster, a noted Vancouver radio personality, "It's a financial invasion. For the first time, the middle and upper classes are feeling like financial midgets."

The backlash against immigration and land speculation by Hong Kong families has found its most stark expression in the schoolyard. Finding a good English-language education for their children, in a less-congested school, is one of the main reasons that many Hong Kong families have emigrated to Vancouver. Kerrisdale is a coveted location for the newcomers for the simple reason that it is home to some of the city's best public and private schools. As the more-established Anglo-Saxon parents grumble over the dinner table about all the negative changes taking place in their neighborhood, their children listen and absorb their prejudices.

One school where the dislocation is particularly acute is Magee Secondary School. A picture hanging in the school's front hall shows that only 36 of the 220 children in the school's 1987-88 graduating class are of Asian descent. But according to the principal, Peter Minichiello, one-third of the 1988-89 student body is Asian, and by the 1989-90 school year, Asian kids will represent at least 50 per cent of the students. Says Minichiello: "Some of the Caucasian children here are resentful. They say that the Hong Kong kids are the only ones getting A and B marks. They feel the hard-working Asians have attained those marks at their expense."

Out in the schoolyard a group of pretty, white, grade-eleven girls have gathered for lunch. As far as they are concerned, the Hong Kong immigrants at the school are not part of their lives.

"They are up on the third floor, where the English-as-a-Second-Language classroom is, and they don't speak English up there," says one girl.

"They don't show up at basketball games," pipes up another. "Perhaps they have no interest in basketball."

"I don't think anybody dates them because you can't communicate with them."

"I have more like a complaint," offers one girl, who seems to exude that I'm-the-most-popular-girl-in-the-class confidence. "All the old houses that we grew up with are going down. They build huge houses and cut down the trees. I have lived here in Kerrisdale since I was five. All my favorite pathways are gone. They tear down the nice houses."

"Yeah, pretty soon every other house will be owned by a Hong Kong family," volunteered another. "They all look like banks. Big and square with no garden or trees."

Inside, the school cafeteria seems to have an imaginary Green Line down the middle. On one side sit the Whites. On the other, the Chinese kids are clustered at their own tables.

"We are so different socially. Most of us are grade elevens and we own cars," says a Chinese boy with a BMW. (A show of hands reveal that five of the ten guys at one table own cars, including Jaguars and BMWs. All the cars cost more than $20,000 each.) "Most of them don't. So our topics of conversation are different. They have different hobbies."

"They insult you harshly when we are showering because physically they are bigger," says one in the Chinese group. "We have to stick together so that they won't pick on us."

"Then they accuse us of being in Asian gangs, which we are not."

"Some of those Canadian girls think our parents deal drugs," says another.

Long-established white Vancouverites claim that they don't hate Chinese people; it's just that the pace of change has left them bewildered and angry. Hong Kong money is shaking Vancouver, the city where west-coast weird meets British bluster, and life-style has always mattered more than enterprise, to the very bottom of its lush roots. The biggest difference is that Vancouver is being forced to do things Asian-style. Downtown developers and construction companies complain that they are not getting their share of the downtown construction action. The city's longer-established citizens are discovering that, like it or loathe it, when house-hunting they can no longer afford to dawdle around the city, picking and choosing just the right place. The present reality is that you buy the first home that meets your needs as quickly as possible — before a fax arrives from Hong Kong. Says David Lam, B.C.'s Chinese-Canadian lieutenant-governor: "Traditional residents are saying 'What can we do? What can we do?' "

The city's concerned elements are already marshaling their troops. Jack Volrich, a former mayor of Vancouver, has co-founded a group called the British European Immigration Aid Foundation which is lobbying for an increase in the number of immigrants from British and European sources. "Thirty years ago, 85 per cent of our immigrants were from Britain, Europe and Australia. Now they are down to only 10 to 15 per cent. At the moment the government is directed toward encouraging immigration from Southeast Asia and people with money," he says. Volrich, who acknowledges that his group derives its resolve from its dislike of "profiteering from residential properties," proposes a number of possible solutions for the problem, among them: charging immigrants in the government's investor class at least $1 million; imposing a land speculation tax on residential properties; and forbidding residential land ownership by non-residents. "It is causing increasing concern to a lot of Canadians, but so many are afraid of speaking out on the issue because they are afraid of being called a racist or a bigot," he says. "Vancouver is a city under a cloud of concern about what its future may be. People don't know where it is leading us."

An extreme sign of the dark undercurrent came in March, 1989, in a notice found tacked to a board in the still-desolate Expo lands awaiting development by Li Ka-shing. It read:

STOP THE SPREAD OF CANCER.
FELLOW CANADIANS:
Wake up before it's too late! Our Government is selling us out by encouraging the infiltration of Chinese, who are buying up our land and raising our taxes. The Chinese population is over one billion and is spreading like wildfire! What about our future and our children's future, culture and opportunities? There will be nothing left for our children, if we don't stop this spread of Cancer. The Government argues, it is good for the country; how? By lining their pockets! Who profits? You can bet it's not us! Look what is happening in China and Tibet, if we want to remain a democratic country; Stand up for your rights now, unite before it's too late!

Patriot
(Put out Asian Takeover . . . Riot)

All this talk has a frighteningly familiar ring to it. Today, Asian money is charting the city's future. Yet, for most of its 103-year history, British Columbia has displayed an attitude of systematic racism toward its Chinese citizens, virtually unrivaled in its virulence by any other community in the country. As sociologist Peter Li concludes in his 1988 book, *The Chinese in Canada*: ". . . except for a few years after the arrival of the Chinese in British Columbia in 1858, the history of the province was marred by a long-lasting anti-Chinese movement. Anti-orientalism was common among politicians, union leaders, white workers, and employers, although each group benefitted directly or indirectly from the presence of the Chinese." Perhaps University of British Columbia sociologist Graham Johnson is right, when he calls the latest cultural backlash against Hong Kong immigrants part of B.C. residents' "predilection to react negatively to other ethnic groups."

British Columbia's development didn't improve the lot of its Chinese citizens. By the time of its incorporation in 1886,

Vancouver, which had sprang up at the western end of the CPR, was a thriving centre with a bustling harbor, rail yard and industries. Chinese workers began to flock to the growing city. But, as Chinese-Canadian archivist Paul Yee recounts in his book, *Saltwater City*, they received a cool reception. Vancouver's newspapers warned that the Chinese presence in the city's business section would lower property values and urged that the Asians be kept out. After the Great Fire of June, 1886, destroyed much of the city, the by-and-large white citizenry passed resolutions to prevent the Chinese re-establishing themselves. "In November a white worker's group known as the Knights of Labour began a campaign to evict the Chinese from Vancouver," recounts Yee. "They ordered stores not to hire Chinese people or sell them food or supplies. Any store defying the boycott found a big white X painted on its sidewalk."

The first widespread anti-Chinese violence occurred in January, 1887, when a contractor arrived to clear the West End forest with twenty Chinese workers. A crowd of 250 whites tore down their camp and herded the crew down to the docks where they were shipped to Victoria. The Chinese returned, and on February 24, another mob tore down the shacks, kicked and beat them and torched their possessions. The next morning the Chinese were loaded on wagons and sent off to New Westminster. But soon they were back again — this time to stay.

Jobs abounded for Chinese labor in Vancouver and, before long, a Chinatown sprang up on the shores of False Creek in the heart of the city. Many of the Chinese toiled in Vancouver's shingle and sawmills and worked as cooks and servants in homes, hotels and logging camps. A number were self-employed, cultivating pig and vegetable farms and opening laundries.

Yet, the racism persisted. On a hot, sultry evening in 1907, Vancouver's 2,000-strong Asiatic Exclusion League staged a parade to call for an end to Asian immigration into Canada. Spurred on by a brass band and banners calling for "A white

Canada and no cheap Asian Labor," the crowd rampaged through the city's Chinese and Japanese quarter, breaking windows and threatening the non-whites. The next day the white crowds returned, trying several times to invade Chinatown again; fortunately, the area was roped off and guarded by police.

Even the introduction of the Chinese Exclusion Act of 1923 did not placate white critics. After the sensational 1924 Janet Smith murder scandal, in which a Chinese schoolboy was wrongfully accused of killing a white maid, Scottish organizations demanded a law forbidding white women and Chinese Canadians from working in the same house. In 1927, the Ku Klux Klan chapter in Vancouver called for governments to end Asian immigration, to send all Asians back overseas and to expropriate their Vancouver property.

Yet, the pioneers persevered, filling jobs shunned by whites in the hope that things would get better. Things didn't. The Chinese Canadians who had come to dominate the city's fresh produce business by the 1920s, were particular targets. By the late 1920s, Vancouver businessmen, who viewed Chinese-Canadian greengrocers as a threat, successfully petitioned Victoria to let municipal governments limit the number of shops owned by non-whites. Chinese-Canadian cafe owners were also under fire as a result of the Women and Girls Protection Act of 1924, which allowed the police chief to force employers to discharge white females from work that damaged their moral fibre — the police alleged that the Chinese turned the young white women into prostitutes.

The first generation of Chinese Canadians who grew up in the city's Chinatown faced a grim future. Many of them had been educated in Canada — some even attending university — but racial discrimination made it literally impossible for them to work in the mainstream outside Chinatown. "Those taking medical, dental, or other professional degrees looked to China for work," wrote Paul Yee. "In general, young men went to work in cafes, laundries or grocery stores. They were waiters, they drove taxis and trucks, they booked aboard steamships and they worked in lumberyards. The options for women included cannery work, clerking in grocery stores, or sewing at Charles Chan Kent's garment factory, which was the only operation of its size run by Chinese Canadians."

When World War Two began, B.C. politicians did not even want to draft Chinese Canadians into the armed forces for fear that they would then demand the right to vote. In the summer of 1944, Chinese Canadians were drafted only because of a manpower shortage and because other Canadians complained that the Chinese were being treated preferentially.

When the young Chinese Canadians returned from the war, public opinion had swung over to their side. As the Canadian immigration policy changed in the post-war period, Vancouver's Chinese community experienced a renaissance of sorts, which saw their numbers double to 15,000 from 1951 to 1961. Once the communists shut down the Chinese borders in 1949, Hong Kong became the main source of the influx. At the same time, wives and children of long-separated families were arriving under the new rules, the birth rate was climbing and Chinese from elsewhere in Canada flocked to Vancouver.

Most headed for Chinatown. But a so-called Chinese Shaughnessy also sprang up where a number of wealthy Chinese families lived. At the same time, Chinese Canadians began to penetrate the ranks of professions such as law, pharmacy and medicine. In 1957, ninety-nine years after the first Chinese was thought to have settled in Canada, lawyer Douglas Jung became the first Chinese Canadian elected to Parliament, representing Vancouver Centre.

A new era began a decade later when Ottawa finally altered its immigration rules to eliminate discrimination on the basis of race or nationality once and for all. Suddenly, aggressive immigrants who had learned to compete in the highly competitive

Asian marketplace began pouring into Chinatown, overwhelming the descendants of the pioneers and the families reunited
during the 1950s.

The first wave of monied immigration headed for Vancouver
in 1967, after Hong Kong was rocked by pro–People's Republic
of China riots. Another wave began in 1972, when the stock
market bottomed out and the colony was flooded with Vietnamese refugees. Hundreds of millions of dollars poured into
the city during these years, but raised little concern because the
money was quiet and conservative. That all changed when the
big buying spree began in 1982, when communist China began
to negotiate with Britain about relinquishing control over the
colony. Hong Kong's new monied elite had, by and large,
become wealthy speculating in local real estate during the
booming 1960s and 1970s. Now, they were looking for insurance, and what better place than Vancouver with its large
Chinese community, nearness to the huge U.S. market and
even its close physical resemblance to Hong Kong?

Vancouver, it turned out, never knew what hit it. The city
was caught off guard by the Asian interest in its residential and
commercial property, and the resulting real estate boom. By
1989, even the B.C. government realized that things were starting to get out of control — but it was a problem of their own
making. Since Expo 86, the right-wing Social Credit government has been willing to do just about anything to attract Hong
Kong money. Its province's Hong Kong office has a squad of
bureaucrats on hand to help smooth the path into Canada for
monied immigrants. The B.C. Chamber of Commerce also has
an office in Taipei. At the same time, there's been a steady flow
of bureaucrats and Socred politicians from B.C. courting the
new wealth. Finance minister Mel Couvelier made three official
trips to Asia during 1987-1989. A $2 million program funded by
the federal and B.C. governments, called the Asia–Pacific Initiative, was launched to explore ways to promote the province as

the gateway to Canada. The Vander Zalm government even re-jigged the investor immigration rules, approving a new vehicle which allows investors to qualify for entrance by putting their money into an office building or commercial development, as long as it is outside Vancouver. At the time of writing, John Jansen, B.C.'s Minister of International Business and Immigration, was pressing the federal government to further broaden the choices of real estate investments that are eligible for immigration purposes.

The Socred pitchmen haven't fared too badly. Many of the newcomers have net worths of $10 to $15 million. That makes them middle class by Hong Kong standards, but by the standards of contemporary Vancouver, they are extremely rich. When the situation demands it, they can be extremely patient investors, waiting years for investments to pay. But when the situation warrants, they make deals with a swiftness that leaves Vancouver's more plodding business people shaking their heads in disbelief. Usually, the Hong Kong immigrants are family capitalists who work closely with members of their large, extended clan. The same, of course, can be said of Toronto's new breed of Chinese entrepreneur. But, because of the uproar their presence has caused, Vancouver's Asian business circle is even more close-knit, and its members often deal only with associates from their own country.

For proof of their unity, visit the elegant Li Pai Lau seafood restaurant, located smack dab at the main intersection of Kerrisdale's new Chinese neighborhood. It has become the haunt of the Hong Kong rich and powerful, who talk business over abalone and Chinese mushroom soup, braised chicken, and salmon in black-bean sauce. The night we dined there, a flashy red sportscar owned by Patrick Tse, the movie-star–turned–garment-factory-owner, glittered in the restaurant parking lot. Inside, Tse, his wife, Deborah, James Cheng, a Vancouver architect favored by Hong Kong clients, and Geoffrey Lau, a developer whose family has more than $100 million in Canadian assets, including the new Coopers & Lybrand building opposite Vancouver's old CPR station, were entertaining in a private banquet room. The guest of honor: a man who had flown here to make a bid on the Hotel Vancouver, but ended up involved in a joint venture hotel-office building deal, and buying what had once been B.C. entrepreneur Nelson Skalbania's sumptuous Vancouver mansion for $4.7 million.

Hong Kong money is coming to Vancouver in all sizes, shapes and sexes. Among them are the so-called astronauts, who set their families up in big homes in South Granville, Richmond or Kerrisdale, and then commute to Hong Kong for business. Others have taken the plunge, moving their families and their vast wealth to Vancouver outright, and simply picking up where they left off in Hong Kong.

Still others are fresh-faced twenty- or thirty-year-olds, deployed to Vancouver by the more conservative older generation, to diversify the family fortunes, and pave the way for the rest of the clan. Victor Li is a prime example of this phenomenon. His status as a Canadian — he studied engineering here — was instrumental in his father's 1986 takeover of Calgary-based Husky Oil Ltd. Politicians tried to quash the deal as a foreign foray into the local energy industry, but failed because Victor was part of the transaction. And, despite his problems over the Expo lands, Li fits the mold of the Chinese super-rich who usually like to operate quietly and privately in Vancouver, attracting public attention only when they buy a city landmark for the family portfolio.

Few are as wary of the spotlight as Caleb Chan, who controls more than $100 million of B.C. real estate. Sitting in his eleventh floor boardroom in the $32-million Burrard Building, which he owns, in downtown Vancouver, Chan anxiously shuffles his expensive black leather loafers and is visibly uncomfortable in the presence of a reporter with a tape recorder. "I just don't like it. I really don't like to talk to the press," says the short, slight, thirty-seven-year-old. "I have had some bad experiences. *News-week* called me 'an Oriental Rothschild.' What does that mean? It sounds like some kind of wine. My problem is that I like a low profile but my projects are high-profile."

He has a point. In the fall of 1988, his company, Burrard International Holdings, spent $40 million to buy Vancouver's historic Georgia Hotel from mainland Chinese interests. The Eugenia condominium tower which he is erecting along prestigious Beach Avenue, overlooking Stanley Park, set a new price record for condominium sales in the city — a whopping $400 per square foot — and the sixteen condo units are listed at more than $1.2 million apiece. As well, Chan is developing two condominium projects at the Whistler ski resort worth about $20 million each.

Chan made a fortune in San Francisco, handling properties for his family, which once owned one of Hong Kong's largest garment companies. After the family business was sold in 1986, Chan, and his brother, Tom, left for Vancouver where property prices had been in a slump for years, in some cases losing one-third of their value. Their timing was impeccable. "The Canadian dollar was undervalued. And they were beginning to talk about this free trade thing which we knew would help the dollar," recalls Chan, who has an MBA from the University of Californa, Berkeley. Moreover, Canada had begun to roll out the red carpet for Asian immigration, which meant that Vancouver had the potential to become an important centre for Pacific Rim money.

Today, Chan is a fixture among the young, hip, Hong Kong crowd which has sprung up in Vancouver. He likes to ski, windsurf and ride the Pacific breakers when he can get good waves. "I just want to drive a station wagon and wear jeans, just be an ordinary guy," he says. But Chan will never be an ordinary guy. Outside of B.C., he still owns a string of substantial properties in the U.S., including a resort condominium at Lake Tahoe, and San Francisco's Ramada Renaissance, the city's third-largest hotel, with 1,000 rooms. Chan, in fact, has not even applied for Canadian citizenship, preferring to operate on a work visa in Vancouver, a decision that he says reflects his belief that U.S. property is more stable than Canadian.

David Ho, like Caleb Chan and Greta Garbo, just wants to be left alone. As he pilots his gold, custom-made $250,000 Ferrari Testa Rossa over Vancouver's Granville Bridge, weaving between three lanes of traffic, Ho seems an unlikely recluse. The car appears only rarely on Vancouver streets, and when it does, it is followed by hoots and whistles of approval from admiring onlookers. Yet, Ho seems to get little joy from his Ferrari. In three years he has clocked less than 1,000 kilometres on it. He particularly dislikes driving it during daylight because of the attention it attracts. Indeed, when the car pulls up to a stoplight during a rare, mid-afternoon drive, he squirms in his seat as passersby stop and stare. Usually, he only takes the car out in the wee hours of the morning, for maintenance runs around the empty streets near the University of British Columbia. His modesty is also evident when he allows the United Way to raise money by offering rides on his "Miami Vice"–style forty-two foot Executioner open-sea racing boat. Newspaper photographs of the event identify him only as "David (in dark windbreaker)" and organizers simply describe him as someone they hired to drive the boat.

But Ho, whose family made its fortune in tobacco, remains a prime example of how Hong Kong money is providing new jobs and industrial development in B.C., not just speculating passively in the real estate market. After paying $100 million for Gray Beverage, a soft drink bottling company and Pepsi franchise holder, he spent $24 million to build a 310,000-square-foot high-tech plant and head office for it in Delta, B.C. The run-down sixty-year-old UBC Golf Club underwent a similar facelift after he bought it for $30 million. He spent $5 million to build a

15,000-square-foot clubhouse housing two restaurants, three banquet rooms, a pro shop and generously proportioned changing facilities, including foot baths in the washrooms. Ho also built a public driving range adjacent to the clubhouse, a variety of new waterholes for the eighteen-hole course, and a floral garden and gazebo designed to attract wedding parties.

An overweight chain-smoker, whom one friend described as "just a rich kid playing with his parents money," Ho is endlessly fascinated by high-tech toys. His office telephone, like the one in his home, is part of an electronic desk pad that includes a clock, calculator and a new Meridian phone that can be programmed to play a tune of his choice instead of ringing. Behind the desk is a high-voltage electrode plasma sphere that emits multi-colored volts when touched — a popular desk toy. And on a side table is a history of the Ferrari company signed by Enzo Ferrari. Yet, though he lavishes money on personal luxuries, he is always looking for ways to trim operating costs. When he takes his own van through the on-site carwash belonging to Gray Beverage and intended for the delivery fleet, he spends five minutes grilling an employee to find out if the wash cycle can be shortened to save water and soap. And, rather than scrap antiquated or rusty Pepsi vending machines, he refurbishes them to dispense Gray Beverage products. Says his wife, Rita: "Just like at home. He buys several pairs of identical socks so that if one sock of a pair wears out, he replaces just one instead of both." As Ho says: "A penny is a penny."

The Hong Kong entrepreneurial drive is infectious and affects everyone it touches — even Kwai Cheong (Casey) Liu, who, at sixty-eight, saddles up his red thoroughbred, Sundance, each morning, for a two-hour ride down the country trails around Vancouver's Southlands. Liu, who has swept-back black hair, amused eyes, and an overbite, is one of the growing number of Hong Kong retirees who have recently emigrated to Vancouver. But the active horseman, golfer, skier and hunter is far from retiring. Since arriving in Vancouver, he has "dabbled" in real

estate development, building two condominium towers downtown, and a row of luxurious houses, known as The Jardine
Houses, in the upscale West Side that he subsequently sold for
$800,000 each.

Liu is not one of the heavyweights in Vancouver's development game. For one thing, his projects are located beyond the
prime core of the city. According to one architect, Liu also
dawdles and is indecisive, perhaps because he is content with
the money he has already made through his prosperous garment
company in Hong Kong. Vancouver real estate is only a hobby
for his retirement years. "You tell them I never calculate how
much I worth," he says, looking over his half-glasses. "I only
know how much I owe the bank. I am very humble, like
retirement gentleman. But retirement has lots of opportunity in
Vancouver, because much prosperity here."

You don't have to tell Ernest Hui that. His family began buying
and developing Vancouver property in the 1970s. Today they
own the Georgian Towers overlooking Stanley Park, condos in
the resort towns of Whistler and Coquitlam and retail and office
towers in Vancouver and Richmond. Even so, Ernest, who is in
his late thirties, keeps spinning deals. Consider how he added a
paddlewheeler and floating restaurant to his country club, ma-
rina and public market project in Richmond, B.C. That enabled
him to call the development a tourist attraction instead of a real
estate development, which meant it qualified under the
province's investor immigration rules. "And by doing that, part
of the project qualifies as a vessel, which turns it into a tax
shelter," says Ernest gleefully. The whole project will cost about
$90 million, including the necessary twenty-five acres of water-
front land and the paddlewheeler which, not surprisingly, was
purchased in Hong Kong.

Lucy Shaw, a pipe-smoking Cathay television producer-cum-
real estate developer, also comes from old money. In Hong

Kong, her family name means theatres, movie stars and Holly-wood-style productions. In its heyday, the Shaw Brothers Studio, owned by her movie mogul uncle Sir Run Run Shaw, produced forty-five to fifty films a year and distributed them around the world. In 1984 the Shaws decided that there was more money to be made in film distribution than in production. Now the company produces publications, including a widely circulated TV guide. Sir Run Run is now chairman of TVB, the television station that has 80 per cent of the Hong Kong market. And Lucy, who left Hong Kong in 1963 for the United States, and became a Canadian citizen three years later, is building a deluxe townhouse condo project on a hunk of prime property on West Georgia Street, right across from Stanley Park. "Canada is underpopulated," says the soft-spoken forty-year-old as she stuffs fragrant tobacco leaves into the bowl of her pipe with a nicotine-stained finger. "They have to have immigrants. And the Asians are the group that will have education, entrepreneurial spirit and money."

Today, the majority of Vancouver's 150,000 Chinese are new immigrants, and on the streets of Chinatown, the past and future walk side-by-side. The central artery is Main Street, which is anchored — literally and symbolically — by an elaborate, early-twentieth-century stone building which houses the Canadian Imperial Bank of Commerce and by, the modern, glass-faced HongKong Bank of Canada building. Running the length of Main Street are shops, most of them owned by recent Hong Kong immigrants, selling fashions, jewelry, tapes of Chinese music and fresh foods. Even in winter, shopowners keep their storefronts open so that the bottles of herbs and twisted roots, fatty meats, dandelion leaves and collard greens spill out onto the street. "Oh you cannot imagine the fresh bread and rolls with barbecued meat," enthuses a Chinese cabdriver in his fifties, as he points out his favorite Chinese cake shop. At Hon's Wun Tun House you can get a filling lunch for $2.25. At Kam Tong Enterprises Ltd., there is an array of meats and raw and cooked fish. Nearby is Yuen Fong, Chinatown's oldest grocery store. At Kiu Shun Trading Co., a herbal store, you can get deer's horn, which is used to increase blood circulation in elderly people. "But if you are young, do not try it," warns the driver. "You will bleed and have to go to the hospital."

And yet, there's a noticeable tension between the new and the old. Resentment of the newcomers' vast wealth is no doubt part of it. But the established Chinese families are also worried that they are being tarred with the same brush as the controversial new immigrants. If you want a metaphor for this internecine conflict, none is probably better than the huge financial, shopping, office and hotel project which is slated for Li Ka-shing's Expo lands development, an area that lies adjacent to Chinatown and could threaten its commercial base. Our cab-driver turns cold at the mention of the recent wave of Hong Kong immigrants. "They make our lives harder," he says. "They bring their money and buy a brand-new house and car. We work every day and don't have either. They only think of themselves. Yeah, Hong Kong people are making money for Hong Kong people."

Nobody understands the complex conflicts raging through Vancouver better than David Lam, real estate tycoon, philosopher, philanthrophist and lieutenant-governor of British Columbia since September, 1988. You only have to meet the jowly, bespectacled sixty-five-year-old to know that he is not the retiring figurehead of monarchy who normally occupies the lieutenant-governor's post in most Canadian provinces. While most shy away from controversy, Lam has made it his personal crusade to bridge the widening rift between the white community and the new Asian investors. "I do not see myself as the representative of Hong Kong, or the spokesman for Hong Kong groups or for a visible minority. As the Queen's representative I am for everyone," he says sitting in his Oriental antique-decorated penthouse overlooking Stanley Park. "I have to be above politics and above controversies. Unfortunately, it is not me to just be seen, and cut ribbons and have my pomp. I want to tell as many people as possible the messages from my heart about healing, reconciliation and love."

David Lam is a worldly, elegant, deeply religious man who grew up in a devout Baptist family in Hong Kong. He attended university there, in Canton and in Philadelphia, Pennsylvania, before returning to his birthplace where he ran a small bank for eighteen years. Looking out his window which is dominated by a large ceramic giraffe that sits on the floor, he enthusiastically describes the seed catalogues that he used to read on the sly in his classroom in Hong Kong in order to learn English. "For a penny, I could buy six old seed catalogues. I would learn to read the beautiful names: King Alfred trumpet lily, tulip, hyacinth. Oh my, they were beautiful! One day the teacher caught me with it. He thought it would be a dirty magazine. He could not believe I was reading a seed catalogue."

Lam and his wife, Dorothy, first saw Vancouver during a ten-day holiday in 1960. Seven years later they moved there for good, motivated, according to Lam not by money but by the city's overwhelming beauty. In any event, he crammed his family into a single motel room in Vancouver while he looked for work during the day, and learned real estate appraisal at night. His contacts back in Hong Kong served him well. He soon prospered, selling real estate to offshore buyers, working first for Wall & Redekop Realty Ltd., later forming Canadian International Properties Ltd. By the time he retired in 1982, he had funneled an estimated $500 million of Hong Kong money into North America, and built a personal fortune exceeding $100 million in the process.

Lam, in fact, still has extensive real estate holdings, including an $82-million downtown office building in San Francisco, a shopping centre in Arizona and the Vancouver apartment building. But he likely won't have them for long. A few years ago he sold a San Francisco building for $21.5 million and turned the proceeds into the Lam Foundation, from which he donates $1 million a year to charity. So far Lam's money has enriched the University of British Columbia Management Research Library, University of Victoria Asian Centre, Simon Fraser University, Regent College library and Sun Yat-Sen Classical Chinese Garden in Vancouver's Chinatown. He also has taken out a $5-million life insurance policy that will go to a variety of charities upon his death. Said Lam: "My wife and I lead a simple life. My motor home and my sailboat are my only toys."

Lam, if the truth be known, was an inspired appointment. As a Hong Kong–born Canadian who had made, as he says "a few dollars in real estate," and is now in the process of giving them back to society, he has clout with major Hong Kong investors and with the mainstream British Columbian. Indeed, news of his appointment was greeted with joy in Hong Kong and brought hundreds of offshore congratulatory telegrams. During our conversation, Lam was in a state of high excitement because, that evening, he was scheduled to attend a UBC fund-raising dinner at which he would announce that he had just convinced a major Hong Kong "mystery man" to donate $10 million to the university.

The growing conflict in Vancouver worries him deeply. That is why he has chosen to "talk to the people" in an effort to defuse the tension. Publicly and privately he has implored established B.C. residents for understanding. "It is quite natural for people to see someone who is visibly different and to feel uncomfortable — this is human," he says. "But that feeling can develop into avoidance, resistance, a battleground. I urge people to pick a common ground rather than a battleground." In a March 11, 1989, speech Lam told the Canadian Club that Canadians must show patience with the newcomers, even if some are "ruthless and money-obsessed. We have invited them. They will help us if we guide them, if we cultivate them properly."

In fact, he claims that Hong Kong investors, who account for only about one-third of demand for Vancouver residential housing at the moment, are not the main reason for the city's housing crunch. "The key is to increase supply," he says. During the March, 1989, throne speech, he outlined one possible incentive program to increase supply, a building fund in which the Socred government would help to subsidize construction of rental or senior citizens' housing.

At the same time, he has bluntly warned Asian investors not to speculate in B.C. residential property, taking particular aim at those who buy rental homes and then turf out the tenants so that they can put up bigger houses that sell for a big profit. "No amount of goodwill, Christian and Confucian talk, will heal that hurt and pain." Whenever possible, Lam also tells Hong Kong people not to build a wall around themselves and to become involved in community affairs. "It is not the Great Wall mentality of China that I want. I would rather build bridges. They must understand B.C.'s neighborly values and environmental heritage. If Hong Kong immigration means Hong Kongization, then the price to B.C. will be prohibitive."

But, even Lam's heartfelt words can't relieve the strain. Perhaps, as one observer says, the conflict is simply too fundamental to be easily quelled. Essentially, the British Columbia government is trying to convince Asian investors not to do what comes naturally: operate together and speculate in a real estate market that just gets hotter and hotter. Just as difficult, is to persuade established Vancouverites to welcome a group of foreigners that is too reluctant to adapt to the ways of their new-found home, and too willing to transform into their own image the city that welcomed them.

7/ BUILDING A CAPITALIST BRIDGE

He exists in a curious limbo, living in three very different worlds thousands of miles apart, but calling none of them home. Stephen Yeung — phenomenally tall and even leaner than most Chinese males — spends about a third of his time in rollicking Hong Kong, where he runs a burgeoning stable of building companies and lives alone in an elegant condominium in the New World Centre, in the heart of Central. Almost daily, a chauffered limousine bearing a special visa licence whisks the former electrical engineer across the border of Canton into the Shenzhen Special Economic Zone, where his companies have been busy since the early 1980s working for the government of the People's Republic of China. When there's nothing pressing in Hong Kong or China, he heads to Hong Kong International Airport and flies to Toronto, where his wife, Lai-Chu, and three children, Sandy, May and Stephenson, have lived since 1984, in a house in the city's Port Union area.

Yeung is a so-called astronaut, one of the growing number of Hong Kong rich who log thousands of miles yearly jetting back and forth between their business bases in Asia, and their families and businesses in Toronto and Vancouver. Sometimes, as in the case of Lucina Ho, casino-magnate Stanley Ho's wife, it is the wife and children who immigrate to Canada while the husband continues to live in Hong Kong. In other cases, businesses are split between couples. This is the situation of Julia Chen who runs the Golden Bull Restaurant in Toronto, while her husband runs the acclaimed restaurant of the same name in Hong Kong. Then there are people like Dorothy and Peter Tsang, who own a telecommunications company in Hong Kong, and a company that imports portable cellular telephones to Canada. While they both call Toronto home, Peter disappears for long stretches of time to supervise the bread-and-butter business in Hong Kong.

Their motivations vary. By straddling East and West, some are hoping to cultivate the best of both worlds: Hong Kong's opportunities for huge and rapid-fire financial returns, and Canada's promise of security and long-term prosperity. Others are so uncertain about their chances for success in Canada that they delegate family members to run the Canadian operation, while they tend to their profitable Hong Kong operations, until their North American businesses become viable. Whatever the reasoning, there is no shortage of Chinese immigrants who obtain Canadian citizenship and then catch the first flight back to Hong Kong. This fact is showing up almost daily in the colony's maternity wards, where new Canadian citizens are being born. It is estimated that ten babies are born in Hong Kong each month to parents with Canadian citizenship — most of them astronauts. When he flys back to Hong Kong to meet with clients, Toronto realtor Frank Chau recognizes whole flights full of the country-skipping businessmen, all with Canadian passports safely tucked away in their suit pockets.

Back in Canada, these long separations are taking their toll on the divided families who live in so-called superhomes in some of the richest suburbs in Canada. "A lot of wives left behind in

Canada are very understanding," says Chau. "As long as the
husband gives financial and spiritual support, they will not
pressure them to make a disclosure." Still, wives commonly
urge their husbands to invest heavily in Canada when they first
immigrate, so that if a divorce occurs, they have a better claim on
the family assets.

These continent-hopping men and women are actually the
bricks and mortar of the human and financial bridge that is
being built between Hong Kong and Canada. Stephen Yeung,
who is only in his early forties, is a prime example of how this
will happen. Few people bridge the gap between Asia and
Canada as well as the serene, elegantly dressed Hong Kong
native. After cutting his teeth in the world's toughest marketplace, he has built an impeccable business reputation in
Beijing, which is displaying a growing willingness to let Hong
Kong businessmen show them the ins and outs of the capitalist
world. Yeung, in fact, is a director of Great Wall International
Investment (Canada) Ltd., one of the 180 subsidiaries of the
state-run Shenzhen Special Economic Zone Development Co.,
which is leading the growing Chinese investment push in Canada. Since early 1987, Great Wall has invested more than $225
million in real estate development projects in Canada, among
them a $200-million office tower, condominium and trade cen-
tre complex in Toronto's Scarborough. And Yeung, who
speaks English with a heavy Cantonese accent, is also the front
man for more millions from the People's Republic looking for a
home in Canada. In that, he is the wave of the future.

Think of it as a bridge of wealthy people arching high across
the Pacific between Canada and China. As the number of
Canadian Chinese with Hong Kong roots surges ever higher,
Canada's links to mainland China will also grow. And as it does,
Canadian businessmen will be able to exploit that growing
relationship. Here's how. Beijing has increasingly come to view
millions of Chinese expatriates — known among the Chinese as
huaqiao (pronounced "huachao") — as a valuable, if not incalculable, asset. And Canadian businessmen who want to enter

into a joint venture — the primary vehicle for doing business in Hong Kong and China — would be wise to join the *huaqiao* in their return to China. For his part, Li Ka-shing, and his two Canadian sons, will give China's fledgling space industry instant international credibility when the country's space administration launches Li's communication satellite into orbit. Li himself admits that he will soon retire and leave the operation to his sons, Victor and Robert, making them two important keystones in the human and financial bridge over the Pacific.

But are Canadian businessmen aware of this new three-way relationship? While our aerospace industry looks south to the Pentagon and U.S. space program for contracts, perhaps they should be examining the viability of teaming up with Li to help the Asian giant build its telecommunications and space program. As Nova Corporation's Bob Blair has shown, such partnerships can be an extremely lucrative strategy. Imagine the rewards for a Canadian communications giant like Northern Telecom Ltd. if it could be involved in wiring a country of one billion people with the latest in telecommunications technology! And this is just the tip of the iceberg. Canadian businessmen, who in some ways pioneered the development of cable television systems in North America, should also be aware that Li will likely land the contract to install cable television in Hong Kong. It would be the largest installation program of its kind in world history, and it can be argued that no country has more expertise in the field than Canada.

Obviously, this Hong Kong- and 1997-driven Chinese migration will open vast opportunities for Canadians wanting to crack open the Asian market, a commercial sector that many economists believe will ultimately dwarf Japan and other Asian giants. In turn, this will open other markets in the Pacific Rim through a far-flung network of ethnic and family contacts that are increasingly anchored in Canada. Perhaps Nova's Robert Blair truly put it into perspective when, during the Calgary reception for Li Ka-shing, he forecast that the amount of investment flooding out of the Pacific Rim into Canada will some day surpass even the flow of financing from the U.S. to Canada. Canadian businessmen should be ready to tap it.

The exodus from China really began during the upheavals of the 1940s, first with the Japanese invasion and then the communist revolution. Today, Chinese emigres dominate the economy of almost every Asian country that they now call home. Canadian businessmen should realize that they will likely do the same in Canada. Some of these same people are now numbered among the richest men in the world. They control vast fortunes in rice, rubber, sugar and almost every bank in Southeast Asia. A number of these families also operate in Canada where they control billion-dollar fortunes, primarily invested in real estate, to which they add every year. Even now, they are poised to break away from investing just in land in order to purchase major trust companies and build high-tech computer manufacturing companies in this country.

Potentially even more significant is the fact that owners of these giant fortunes have maintained close links to the motherland. Consider Taishan province surrounding the Pearl River delta: today it has a population of 800,000, but another 1.2 million of its citizens live abroad. Since China adopted its so-called open-door economic policy in 1979, hundreds of former residents of Taishan, who left to build spectacular fortunes, have returned to build hundreds of miles of paved roads, and dozens of schools. So long as China can demonstrate that its new Liberal economic policies are indeed unshakeable, the flood of money back into China will become a tidal wave, as the expatriates return to assist its development.

According to a *Financial Times* of London survey, officials in Canton, the capital of China's booming Guangdong province, estimate that Cantonese Chinese living abroad have financed the building of 2,000 schools, 100 hospitals and literally thousands of miles of roads. Many of the estimated 500,000 Cantonese Chinese now living in Canada will similarly maintain deep emotional links to the Chinese province. And, if the Li family is an example, they intend to build fortunes in this country by helping to pull China out of its economic morass. As they do, the impact on Canada's economy can only be positive, particularly if Canadian businessmen recognize the possibilities and join forces with Li and others as they pull China forward.

How strong will the Hong Kong connection become? The simple answer is, just as large as Canada wants, or perhaps more accurately, will tolerate. In Vancouver, tragically, these limits are already being sorely tested. Ironically, some groups in Vancouver, the city that likes to bill itself as "the Gateway to the Pacific Rim," are complaining that too many former residents of China are showing up at its gates. Even now an association has been formed that is urging the government to slow the growth of Chinese immigration while boosting the number of immigrants from economically stagnant Britain — a country that has virtually no economic significance outside of Europe. But Canada has already carved a unique position in the latest flight from China. There are already some 60,000 Canadian-educated Chinese, and that number is climbing rapidly. The human bridge between China and Canada may one day bond Canada to the emerging Asian giant as much as British immigration linked Canada to the U.K. before that country's sad decline.

But the boom in Canada–China trade will not happen overnight. In fact, even with Hong Kong's booming economy and its supercapitalists leading the way, China's emergence as the new Asian economic powerhouse may still be decades away. Along the way, it could fall backwards into poverty. Its doctrinaire Marxist rulers, who have been out of fashion for just a decade and a half, could re-assert themselves. There are pessimists, or perhaps more accurately, economic realists, who believe that Hong Kong's five million people and bustling economy will have little impact on China's economy and the living standard of its billion people. At best they suggest that Hong Kong will

boost the economies of the Chinese provinces surrounding it —
but little else. Statistically, the numbers appear to be heavily
stacked against a Chinese economic miracle.

One economic model suggests that when a country's per-
capita income is at or below $500 (China's is now somewhere
between $200 and $300) the economy is fundamentally rural
and is dominated by largely impoverished peasants. It is not
until an economy produces a per-capita income of $2,000 that
the farming population is cut in half, and large-scale manufacturing and export-and-import industries bloom. Per-capita income in China has doubled since the communist takeover in
1949, and the Chinese leadership wants to push it to the $2,000-
per-capita threshold — a level achieved by South Korea and
Taiwan in 1987 — as rapidly as possible. It has a long way to go.
Despite its importance on the world stage, China is now about
as rich (again on a per-capita basis) as the African state of Zambia.

While those dismal statistics appear almost impossible to
surmount, China has nonetheless made incredible strides toward the breakway $2,000-per-capita ceiling. China's gross
domestic product (GDP), the value of all goods and services
produced in the country, actually pulled ahead at an astounding
12 per cent a year between 1982 and 1987. But behind these
numbers stand important differences between China and other
developing nations, particularly its neighbors, South Korea and
Taiwan.

In the uncontrolled rush to industrialization in Taiwan and
South Korea, farmers and their families fled to industrial slums
to work in factories. The Chinese, thanks to nearly 2,000 years
of authoritarian rule that was thoroughly anchored to support
of peasants in the countryside, have been able to clamp a far
greater degree of control on the rural population. They have
deliberately forced industrialization to occur across the entire
face of China. By doing this, the Chinese leadership hopes to
maintain rural China's ancient dominance, to preserve its food

supply, and prevent a violent clash between the rapidly indus-trializing coastal cities and the interior. This balance between industry and agriculture has been wrenched back into line in the past, particularly during the Cultural Revolution, when thousands of academics and bureaucrats were banished from the cities and "re-educated" by peasants.

Because of the central government's control over the popula-tion, and its distribution of resources, optimistic economists suggest that China could defy all odds, and become Asia's next economic giant. But, just how big, and how rapidly, do these optimists expect China to grow? Consider this, one froecast suggests that China's economy will be three times the size of the Soviet Union's by the end of the century. Assuming an almost parallel growth rate of 8 per cent, the living standard of China's billion people would be about 82 per cent of that of the Soviet Union's 272 million people — compared to about one third in 1986. Some economists even compare China's startling growth rate to those of such countries as South Korea, Taiwan, Sin-gapore and even Hong Kong during the 1960s. The implications for Canadian business are huge. Because of its vast population, once underway, Chinese growth would be cumulative and ex-plosive. One economist has compared the unleashing of this economic powerhouse to that of an elephant leading a charge of smaller animals.

The task of raising one billion people out of poverty is as fragile an exercise as it is cruel. In April, 1989, as Hong Kong's mil-lionaires watched nervously, Beijing was hit by a wave of unrest that provided China's more conservative rulers with the oppor-tunity to call for end to economic reforms, effectively slamming the door on ten years of increasingly open economic practices, and raising nagging doubts about the future of Hong Kong following 1997.

Indeed, the violent crackdown on dissidents in Beijing in May, 1989, probably caused hundreds of Hong Kong astronauts to re-read their immigration papers and clutch their insurance policies — their Canadian passports — a little tighter.

Because to the north, students from Beijing's universities began flowing into Tiananmen Square by the thousands. At one point, nearly a million protesters, some chanting slogans and others beating gongs and demanding reform, flooded into the centre of Beijing. These were not radicals bent on toppling the Beijing government. Instead, they were a broad cross-section of working people who wanted to put an end to what they saw as widespread corruption, and the development of what one pro-tester described as a "beautiful, perfect system."

In Hong Kong's boardrooms, the tycoons who oppose demo-cratic reforms in order to keep their fortunes intact, no doubt watched nervously as virtually every sector of Chinese society — students, artisans, white-collar workers, civil servants, jour-nalists, housewives, even soldiers and policemen — joined the demonstration. The Chinese administration, accurately sensing the widespread support for the protesters, waited for seven days, as disorder increased, before they banned further demon-strations, declared martial law and ordered armed troops to clear the square.

At the heart of the struggle were two men who could deter-mine how Canada's growing links to Hong Kong and China develop. As the riots spread, the politburo had to resolve an internal power struggle that pitted the Communist Party's re-formist general secretary, Zhao Ziyang, who is guardian of China's new open-door economic policy, against the more hard-line and doctrinaire prime minister, Li Peng. The forces of economic rule seemed dead when Zhao suddenly capitulated, reportedly offering his resignation. Li declared that conditions of "chaos" and "riot" could no longer be tolerated, and sent motorized columns bearing thousands of troops into the capital. But the demontrators were not easily stopped. In a western suburb of Beijing, 10,000 civilians stopped 100 army trucks carrying 4,000 soldiers.

The supporters of democracy and a more liberal economic policy were buoyed a day later when many of the military vehicles turned back, the soldiers waving in a friendly fashion to the cheering civilians. And later in Tienanmen Square, in what some journalists took to be a salute to the protesters, helicopters buzzed overhead.

For many onlookers from the West, and in increasingly nervous Hong Kong, the rebellion in Tienanmen Square appeared to be a revolution in the making, but it was not. The protesters demanded reform, not the overthrow, of the communist system. In fact, they often marched to the throbbing pulse of the socialist anthem, the "Internationale." According to *Maclean's* magazine, at one point a leader of 3,000 hunger-striking Beijing students struggled upright in his hospital bed with a message for Zhao: "To say that we want to overthrow the party is nonsense. Our intention is to rebuild the prestige of the party among the people."

According to *Maclean's* correspondent Louise Doder, who visited the square daily throughout the week, "the atmosphere was electrifying. With police nowhere in sight, students in red headbands directed demonstrators, and whatever traffic had been able to reach the city centre, through the crowds that choked all the approaches. Whole families hung out of their apartment windows, shouting slogans in support of the students. Many protesters wore T-shirts bearing such familiar Western slogans — in English — as 'We Shall Overcome.' Even some uniformed policemen flashed the V-for-victory sign."

In Hong Kong the mood was pessimistic. What faith Hong Kong businessmen have in the future of the colony evaporated as the struggle in Beijing deepened. As always, life in Hong Kong is reflected in the numbers dancing across the electronic screen high above the trading floor of the Hong Kong Stock Exchange. And the numbers were showing panic as investors, perhaps gazing over their shoulders to the safety of Canada, dumped thousands of shares, sending the market in a deep tailspin. In one day alone the market lost 10 per cent of its value. If that wasn't disconcerting enough for the colony's billionaires, the people of Hong Kong suddenly swept into the streets in support of the Beijing protests. Nearly a million people marched through the financial district to the front door of the New China News Agency — the Chinese Communist Party's official mouthpiece in the colony.

As the marchers rallied, the Hong Kong Stock Exchange's prime barometer, the Heng Seng Index, ended down 339.06, or 10.8 per cent, at 2806.57, the biggest one-day drop since the index plunged more than 30 per cent on October 26, 1987 (after Black Monday). "A lot of people don't have any faith or hope in Hong Kong and that's why there's panic selling," said John Koh, research manager at the Hoare Govett securities house in the colony. The Heng Seng fell to around 2,794 in the first twenty minutes on fears of a government crackdown in Beijing, but recovered to 2,887.89 at midday, partly on unconfirmed rumors that hardline Chinese leader Li Peng would resign. It resumed falling on reports that the army would soon enter Beijing. "The market is entirely driven by uncertainty," said Howard Gorges, director at South China Securities. "If there's good news from Beijing, it could shoot up. If there's bad news, it could fall sharply." But for many investors the bad news will likely continue. Many in Hong Kong have their fortunes inextricably tied to China and greatly fear the idea of political violence there. "There's a feeling either cracked skulls or anarchy are going to emerge," said William Phillips, managing director of Baring Securities. "Neither is good for business."

The agony in Tienanmen Square stood in sharp contrast to the mood that prevailed in Hong Kong in the months leading up to the riots. Indeed, a top lieutenant in Li Ka-shing's empire was so moved by the calmness prevailing in Beijing in the months preceding the demonstration he was moved to say that he saw little difference between a British landlord ruling over Hong Kong, or a communist-Chinese one. Ronald Li, the disgraced former head of the Hong Kong Stock Exchange, complained bitterly that some labor organizations in Hong Kong were trying to wreck the colony's profit-generating system with their demands for reform. One can only wonder how Hong Kong's high-flying capitalists would respond to China's orthodox leaders if they should manage to take firm control and shut down the country's economic reforms. But following the violent events in Tienanmen Square their doubts only increased.

Ultimately, the answer to that question will dictate just how important Hong Kong will become to China, and, as a result, how important Hong Kong immigration will be to Canadian business.

The apparent ascendancy of the conservatives in China shows just how tenuous economic reform and Hong Kong's future is. During a meeting of the Communist Party central committee in September, 1988, Li Peng and his old-guard allies managed to scrap price reforms and other capitalist-style economic reforms. Still they were not entirely successful, and now free-market forces are setting roughly half of all prices in China. But this has led to a somewhat chaotic, two-tier economy. And there are many social problems that, if left unchecked, could lead to a return to strict Marxist principles at a time when Hong Kong's billionaires are hoping that their money-churning forge will be left entirely alone, to be fueled by cheap labor in a totalitarian setting. Indeed, according to *Maclean's*, some of Deng and Zhao's other strategies to open up China's economy to market forces have contributed to a growing gap between rich and poor. In reports filed from Beijing in the tumultuous month of May, *Maclean's* reported: "In Beijing, free-spending entrepreneurs flash their money around in private-enterprise restaurants, where the waitresses are often poor country girls, exploited — and sometimes sexually abused — by their employers."

Barring social upheaval and the closing of China's so-called open-door policy, in the near future, at least, Hong Kong's role in a unified China will probably be limited to raising the economic standards of Chinese provinces and the special economic zones that surround it. While that sounds low-key and even unimportant on paper, it is not. It is here that Canada's growing links to post-1997 Hong Kong and China are taking root.

We have already seen how James Ting, the Shanghai-born Canadian-educated head of International Semi-Tech, inked a three-way deal involving casino magnate Stanley Ho and China, to produce consumer goods and electronics. In the years ahead, Ho and Ting will continue to take advantage of China's vast pool of cheap labor while expanding their computer and consumer products division across North America. It is a feat that could, if Canadian business is adaptable, be repeated over and over after 1997 as Canada's surging population of highly educated Hong Kong Chinese return to Hong Kong to create, maintain or expand their commercial bases.

There is already an astounding number of Canadian companies operating in Hong Kong, and they will be there long after the Chinese replace the British administration. The list reads like a Who's Who of Canadian business. They include: Alcan Asia Ltd., Canada Packers Incorporated, Celanese Far East Ltd., MacMillan Bloedel (Asia) Ltd., Inco Pacific Ltd., Northern Telecom (Asia) Ltd., Seagram (China) Ltd., the Canadian Imperial Bank of Commerce, the Bank of Nova Scotia and the Royal Bank of Canada.

Canadian financial institutions wanting to expand into Asia should follow the model designed in part by the CIBC and D.W. Robbie, vice-president of its Hong Kong operations, a strategy that has put it on a solid footing to expand further into China after 1997. The CIBC has helped some the colony's leading players, such as Li Ka-shing, with financing early in their careers. The contacts solidified as the years went by, and the big

Canadian money house is now seen as the bank with the most expertise in Canadian-Asian finance. In addition to opening branches in China, the CIBC has cultivated contacts with other potential Hong Kong millionaires, by pioneering the use of Hong Kong-based venture-capital funds. Bank officials say they benefit the economy in two ways. By luring Asian investors into their venture funds, they create a built-in market at both ends of the fund: they must sell the funds on the ground in Hong Kong and, once the investor's money is transferred through the investment-fund pipeline to Canada, the investor needs the bank's elaborate web of financial services. The bank hopes that the big payoff will come in the decades ahead, as the CIBC begins to service larger and larger Asian accounts.

The bank is also playing the Beijing card hard. By locating there, Robbie believes the CIBC will be able to bankroll an increasing amount of economic activity in China as the century draws to a close. More importantly, as the economic bridge between Canada, Hong Kong and Beijing forms, the CIBC will be in a position to finance new investment in all countries. Clearly, that fact has not been lost on CIBC's major Canadian competitors who now have aggressive operations in Hong Kong and China.

This country also plays a quiet, but oh-so-typically Canadian, role in Hong Kong: it literally insures the colony. All those familiar bastions of conservative Canada are in Hong Kong and will no doubt be there after 1997: Crown Life Insurance Company, Manufacturers Life Insurance Co. and Sun Life Assurance Co. of Canada. But, as financial deregulation takes hold in Canada, Guangdong will likely be source of much of that activity. In fact, Guangdong, with a spearhead of young Canadian-educated Chinese businessmen operating the economic levers, may already be well on its way to becoming the so-called fifth tiger of Asian economies, surpassing even South Korea and Taiwan. It is already China's largest exporting province, moving

$6 billion in goods in 1987. As it did, it managed to lure $5.3 billion in foreign investment, a whopping 60 per cent of the nation's total.

For years, Vancouver has been the lotus land of Canada, where Easterners come to retire, retreat, savor the smell of lush cedar forest, buy a house overlooking the ocean and possibly get in touch with themselves. Now, however, Vancouverites are more likely to have money and Hong Kong on their minds than self-realization. Vancouver is rapidly joining the ranks of the Pacific Rim centres: San Francisco, Los Angeles, Hong Kong, Singapore and Tokyo. Some real estate developers compare it to California a decade ago, just as Asian money began to flood the city. And as Kurt Vonnegut noted, "We are the Indians now."

But there is an obvious twist to Vonnegut's line: this time the "Indians" can participate fully with their invaders, but that will require a change of thinking by all Canadians, particularly the business community.

Perhaps James Cheng, who designs homes and major developments for some of Hong Kong's richest citizens, can offer insight into how Canadian businessmen can get involved in joint ventures with their new Asian counterparts. In order to link up with the invaders, Canadian entrepreneurs will have to start almost on a social level. Indeed, James Cheng says that the practice of joint venturing in property development, as in the Lee Shau-kee/Cheng Yu-tung deals in Toronto, is "just to have some fun. They do not go out to socialize all that much. But if you do a joint venture with your friends, if forces you to keep up with them. They will say, I'll take 25 per cent and conclude it on a handshake." Thus, for Canadian businessmen turning a deal with a highflying developer from Hong Kong will require a drastic change of habit: fewer lawyers, more trust, and above all, a firm handshake.

Michael Walker, chairman of the right-leaning Vancouver think tank, the Fraser Institute, says that Chinese immigration is exactly what B.C. and Canada needs right now, and Canadian businessmen would be wise to get involved, because there are fortunes to be made — and quickly. According to Walker, Canadian business should view the latest wave of immigrants washing ashore in Canada as an incredible resource, that can make the whole country richer. And joint venturing is clearly the way to go.

There is, in fact, a lot at stake for Canadian business. According to Walker: ". . . we will have to get more and more out of our immigrants from Asia now. The real income levels in Europe have risen so that Europeans are not interested in moving. We probably don't want 'em anyway, because they have the same population bulge. We want younger people, who add to our productive capacity. And the only place to get them is in Asia and Latin America. If we had resisted the immigration of the Guinnesses and the Grosvenors, when they were being driven out of Britain, because of their quaint labor attitudes and their funny Yorkshire puddings, where would we be now? Capital from Hong Kong will free up capital by buying things from people already in Vancouver."

Despite the increasing racism in Vancouver, it is still the city that is attempting to make the growing Chinese community accessible to Canadian businessmen. Businessmen should be aware of two new initiatives that have been launched to court Asian investors. One is the Laurier Institute, formed to examine overseas investment in Canada. Its inaugural dinner in March, 1989, focused on the need for immigration to Canada to slow the country's declining population base. And the second is a joint effort between the federal government and the B.C. government, called the Asia–Pacific Initiative, to explore ways to promote B.C. as the gateway to Canada. Each government is giving $1 million a year to the project.

The two projects should be repeated across Canada, and Canadian businesses, both large and small, should get involved. In Vancouver, clear attempts are being made to turn the west-coast community into an international city worthy of huge investments, by expanding financial, legal and other business services, developing the transportation infrastructure and increasing tourism. Improving the trade and international banking environment is also part of the plan. Vancouver's new International Financial Centre, under the direction of University of British Columbia professor Michael Goldberg, dovetails with that effort, although it was begun before the Asia–Pacific Initiative was approved. Many of the people active on the Initiative's task forces are key figures in the Vancouver Chinese professional community. Andrea Eng, probably the city's most successful realtor; M.Y. Chan, a real estate consultant; and Eugene Kwan, a lawyer with the international law firm Stikeman Elliott, are among them.

Businessmen outside of Toronto and Vancouver can also get involved with Canada's wealthy new immigrants. Indeed, in an effort give Hong Kong immigrants even more incentives to locate in Canada, the B.C. government approved a new vehicle for investor immigration last fall which offers definite joint-venture opportunities. Investors may put their money into building an office building or commercial development, as long as it is outside Vancouver. Just think of the joint-venturing possibilities here! B.C. minister of International Business and Immigration John Jansen said: "The concern is the shortage of housing stock. People from Hong Kong concentrate on urban areas." Jansen and other B.C. officials are also pressing the federal government to broaden other choices of real estate investments that are eligible for immigration purposes. Says Jansen: "We really want to see investment to increase the stock of housing. However, we are concerned that, if we allow investor immigrants to put money into housing developments, the benefit will be temporary. The employment will stop as soon as the house is built."

Canadians hoping to joint venture with the Hong Kong Chinese should follow the example set by a number of Vancouver professional firms that are either hiring or designating experts (often Chinese) to attract Hong Kong business. The rewards flowing from this strategy can be spectacular. One

Vancouver law firm did $400,000 worth of business in the first two months of 1989 alone by having men and women on the scene in Canada and Hong Kong who were able to spot a profitable venture quickly.

Clearly, then, if Canadian business is to be successful in the Asian market they must develop this insight and expertise — and quickly. Eugene Kwan of Stikeman Elliott, whose office walls are dominated by a print of a stylized Buddha, is a typical example. Kwan was four years old in 1950 when he came to Canada with his Hong Kong family. It was a not untypical Canadian beginning for the Kwans. His grandfather started a general store in Victoria that sold canned goods and dry goods. Kwan's father later took over the business, sold it, and returned to Shanghai. Kwan stayed behind and took his law degree at UBC. Today he closely monitors the flow of information to Hong Kong on Canadian real estate deals — a critical job because most major deals are being talked about on the streets of Hong Kong before Canadians even find out.

"Speed," "efficiency" and "adaptability" must be the buzz words driving Canadian business in its dealings with Hong Kong businessmen. This, too, means that businesses will have to bring top Asian Canadians into their companies. Again, Kwan's example is instructive. Kwan's business involves handling the offshore selling of condo units, and advising rich Hong Kong clients on Canadian law and other Hong Kong–related business. The results, as noted above, can be lucrative. Kwan turned over a spectacular hotel deal with a Hong Kong investor in 1989, in which the investor came in on a Thursday, and had bought the hotel by Saturday. Kwan's importance to his firm is underscored by this startling fact: 20 per cent of Stikeman's Vancouver office's business is with Hong Kong clients, and another 10 per cent is with Canadian Chinese.

Like Kwan, John Lee, a chartered accountant with Thorne Ernst & Whinney, is critical to his firm. His presence underscores the innovative expertise that Canadian business needs to develop in its dealings with Hong Kong. Thorne Ernst &

Whinney has six partners assigned to Pacific Rim business, including a tax partner, a mergers and acquisition partner, a Japanese tax partner and three audit partners. Tax advisers like Lee are an essential part of most Hong Kong investors' move across the Pacific to Canada, because many of these potentially rich new citizens are looking for ways to reduce their taxes to the levels in Hong Kong — roughly 17 per cent for corporations.

Next to recognizing the profit-side advantages for Hong Kong business people, their Canadian counterparts must deal effectively with the political subtleties involved. For instance, Lee says that he has not picked up much business by giving seminars in Hong Kong, because he says, people do not want to be seen to be deserting the colony. Equally, it is bad etiquette for a professional to promote the idea of deserting. Most business, therefore, comes through referrals from other lawyers and bankers. Again, developing contacts in Hong Kong is critical for Canadian business. Lee says the ability to move quickly is no less critical, because major investors who suddenly appear in town and want to discuss a major deal do not want to be delayed. Canadian business, therefore, will have to drop its highly regimented, bureaucractic habits if it hopes to tap the flood of Hong Kong money.

But, first and foremost, Canadian entrepreneurs wanting to do business with the rich Asians must learn how to get involved while keeping their potential partner's earnings out of the hands of Revenue Canada. For instance, one of the tax-side maneuvers John Lee uses most often for his clients is, in effect, a five-year tax holiday for new immigrants. The idea is to transfer the immigrant's Hong Kong assets — and that includes anything from shares in an existing Hong Kong company to an expensive coin collection — into a trust. Only after five years, does the income from the investment become taxable. The trust is usually collapsed and the funds patriated to Canada at that time. Lee says such trusts are only worthwhile for immigrants with at least

$1 million to shelter. Any less and it costs to much in administrative fees, but then, what rich Asian immigrant does not have $1 or $2 million to hide from the Canadian taxman?

In the close-knit world of Hong Kong business, deals are often struck over the phone or debated over a bowl of steaming snake soup at such high-level venues as the Hong Kong Hilton. That means that Canadians wanting to do business will have to show up at the table with something more than goodwill and a quick wit. John Lee holds up his end of the power lunches by quickly passing on information to his clients about any number of projects including any number of limited partnerships. He always has a brochure detailing this project or that, ready to go.

Canadian businessmen will have to get used to the idea of dealing with an aggressive group of individuals who are, despite their bullishness, in some extent limited to two business sectors: property and manufacturing. Robert Schultz, who works in the Business Immigration department in the B.C. government, says there is no point encouraging Hong Kong entrepreneurs to get into industries in which they have no skills. "We do not tell them to get into submarine building, space equipment or supplying the Boeing industry in Seattle."

While Canadians have learned to survive under an ever-rising mountain of red tape, the Hong Kong Chinese have not. Any Canadian businessman who can lighten the bureaucratic load will be welcome with business, and more important, access to the always-growing list of rich Hong Kong immigrants. Let's let Ernest Hui, a member of the Hui family that owns Park Georgia Properties in Vancouver, demonstrate how this works, and the type of deal needed to swing it. Hui came to Canada in 1968. Among other interests, he developed a condominium hotel in Whistler, a resort town in a spectacular setting in the Coastal Range, high above Vancouver, which has been largely purchased by Japanese tourists. The Hui family's other businesses in Canada range from a real estate brokerage firm with five branches, a property management, property development and insurance agency. They also own the 202-room Westbrook hotel in downtown Vancouver. Said the high-flying Hui, during an interview in his BMW: "Oh, and we picked up the building next door there, 1200 Hornby. It will either be an expansion of the hotel or an apartment condominium." In typical fashion, Hui had to cut the interview short because he had to spend two days accompanying some visiting investors from Taiwan.

Hui's somewhat shaky BMW might not have impressed his visitors, but his energy would. His office is stacked almost to the ceiling with files and he is always trying to work a new angle on financing. And that is the area that Canadian expertise needs to exploit. Hui, who has a penchant for cutting through regula-tions, has come up with some clever schemes to develop proper-ties that qualify for investor-immigration purposes — as shown in his development of the Richmond, B.C., resort mentioned in the last chapter. The fundamental lesson for Canadian business is this: if you are going to get involved with Chinese business, structure the deal to avoid taxes. It is as simple as that.

Andrea Eng has a good deal to say about how Canadian business can exploit the new Chinese markets. Most important, says Eng, Canadians must be willing to take some risk. She notes that Hong Kong's richest and most powerful developers are often willing to build in Vancouver on a speculative basis, before major tenants have been signed up. Two of Canada's largest real estate firms, for example, had a chance to build major projects in Vancouver, but declined, so opening the door for Hong Kong investors, who immediately moved in. Says Eng: "They are willing to take the risk. Cadillac Fairview was not even willing to build on spec with the Pacific Centre. That is where I think the Hong Kong impact will be in real estate."

Eng has more to tell Canadian business about the practice of joint-venturing among some of Hong Kong's wealthiest individuals: "In Hong Kong, they have government land tenders and recently there was a huge and pricey one. One of our clients, Sun Hung Kai Properties, was bidding against another investor and the price eventually got above $3 billion. So they said, 'Look we're just giving the government money, why don't we do it together?' That's it. They stopped the bidding in fourteen seconds. At the end of the day they are not going to price each other out of the marketplace." Again the upshot for Canadian business is that they will have to learn to act just if they are to wheel and deal with the colony's brightest stars.

Canadian business people often approach Asian businesses as if they were so rich, and Canada such a bargain, that almost any project they propose should fly. Eng says this is a myth that should quickly be put to rest: "They are used to business yields of 20 to 30 per cent, while they pay only 17.5 per cent tax. For them coming to Canada is a diversification process, not a way to escape 1997, and definitely not a bargain." Eng demonstrates the kind of drive Canadians will need to succeed in business with the Asian immigrants. She even makes the time zones work for her: "At the end of my day in Vancouver, I can do all my calls to Hong Kong".

Eng also illustrates how Canadian businesswomen can get along in the male-dominated Asian business world — and again, how their participation will depend on developing contacts. Eng was the first female agent in the commercial real estate firm of Colliers Macaulay Nicolls Inc. and there are still only two women in the company. Says Eng: "Because my family knows people like Mr. Lee Shau-kee, and because I have been working for eight years, I do not have the same kind of barriers as other women might." She adds: "Anyone in Hong Kong who looks at Canadian real estate knows who I am." Eng, who grew up in a family that was constantly talking about real estate, says she consolidated her Hong Kong connections by returning to the colony when the Vancouver market collapsed between 1982 and 1986. The time spent there is now paying lucrative dividends.

It is not just Hong Kong Chinese who are becoming more and more economically important to Canada. Across the nation, from vast ginseng gardens in British Columbia's verdant interior valleys, to hotel developments in suburban Toronto, there is growing evidence that communist Chinese firms are following their Hong Kong cousins to Canada and pressing deeper and deeper into the Canadian market. In recent years, public attention has focused on the billions of dollars pouring into Canada from major Hong Kong investors. But increasingly, and almost invisibly, the state-owned corporations from mainland China are becoming active participants in the Canadian economy. They are searching for expertise, new markets, raw materials and much-needed foreign exchange. And this fact, if Canadian business recognizes it, is also opening up lucrative new opportunities for Canadians. Increasingly, Canada is seen as a training ground for young Chinese executives. And investment in Canada from China in the period from 1980 has amounted to some $500 million, as Chinese firms push deeper into the Canadian real estate and resource sectors.

This is a sudden, and potentially lucrative departure for the Chinese corporations. Until recently, most mainland Chinese enterprises in Canada would only enter joint ventures with established Asian companies familiar with the North American market. But now, in keeping with China's open-door economic policies, an increasing number of companies are going it alone in North America. A number are even following the lead of aggressive Hong Kong entrepreneurs by gambling that huge profits can be made by speculating on real estate in the volatile, but incredibly rich, Toronto and Vancouver real estate markets — a fact that would have appalled their bureaucratic masters only a few short years ago. So far, despite some evidence that the real estate markets in Toronto and Vancouver are rapidly cooling, their bets have been paying off. Says Chen Wenjing, commercial secretary at the Consulate of the People's Republic of China in Ottawa: "The future for us here is very bright."

This new bullishness on Canada is a sudden and growing phenomenon that will likely explode when Hong Kong is turned back to China in 1997. Historically, trade between Canada and China has been a one-way street. For instance, in 1988, Canada exported $2.6 billion worth of goods to China, and imported only $1 billion. In fact, Canada has always had a huge trade surplus with China because of the Asian giant's appetite for wheat, rubber and plastic materials. But that situation is changing. China's recent policy, encouraging a growing exchange of capital and technology with foreign countries, has led Canadian companies to sign agreements during the last quarter of 1988 for the sale of $300 million worth of high-technology projects to China, including giant electric generators and telecommunications equipment.

For its part, China, which until recently targeted nearly all its offshore investment for Hong Kong and the United States, is now accelerating its investment in Canada. At present, forty mainland Chinese companies have set up operations in Canada, more than half of them located in B.C. Analysts say that the Chinese firms in Canada, which operate in a manner similar to Canadian Crown corporations, are now spending heavily to expand their operations. As they do, they are investing in a wide range, even an odd grab bag, of Canadian businesses. These include, fox-breeding operations, the ginseng farms, soft-drink factories and Chinese clothing and furniture marketing outlets.

Canada is benefiting in other ways from this sudden boom in Chinese-Canadian commerce. As the number of Chinese firms operating in Canada increases, they draw support from a wide range of Chinese companies that cater to them. Just a few years ago finding a communist-Chinese service industry in Canada was almost impossible. But now, Air China, for one, targeted the sudden growth in passenger demand between Canada and China in 1988, and launched a regularly scheduled air service to Canada. Now the Bank of China plans to get directly involved in the expansion of Chinese firms in Canada and is applying for a licence to open a number of branches across Canada. The impact of this latter development should not be underestimated by Canada's financial sector, which is now under severe pressure to compete for markets. (Until the deregulation of the domestic financial sector which has taken place under the Conservatives, Canadian banks were under so such pressure. But no more.)

Canadian bankers can expect stiff competition from the Bank of China — the forty-sixth-largest bank in the world. The fact that when the bank's futuristic new headquarters opens in Hong Kong, it will not only be the tallest structure in the colony, but across Asia as well, is more than symbolic. China wants the bank to be leading the leading financial backer of Chinese business around the world. Canadian businessmen in the financial sector, would therefore be wise to join the Bank of China when it arrives in Canada, to participate in joint investments with it. As the CIBC's Hong Kong experience clearly shows, getting in early can pay big dividends later.

As it is with most Chinese business initiatives in Canada, Hong Kong is always involved. Jackson Wang, who oversees the Hong Kong, mainland Chinese and Taiwan markets for B.C.'s Ministry of International Business and Immigration, says that a full 50 per cent of the communist-Chinese companies coming to Vancouver are branches of firms that the People's Republic of China have set up in Hong Kong. He estimates that investments in B.C. alone from China now total at least $100 million. And more than just the profit motive underscores the communist Chinese business boom. Wang says the mainland Chinese firms are often looking for new investments in Canada because they are deeply troubled by the thought of sending their hard-earned profits back to China — only to have them swallowed up by government. Indeed, it is to avoid that result that Chinese firms decided to locate in Hong Kong in the first place.

Now, as an alternative to Hong Kong, these would-be-capitalist communist executives are finding new investments to make in Canada. That has led to some terrible and sometimes comical results. Wang says many of the Chinese delegations interested in entering British Columbia come with only a fuzzy idea of how to launch a successful firm in North America. For example, he recalls how one Chinese company was set up in B.C. simply to negotiate grain prices with the Canadian Wheat Board — a job that the Chinese consulate could have handled just as well. Says Wang: "There is no way we can tell them not to come."

China's ambitions, for the employees of state firms that it sends to Canada often pose insurmountable marketing problems. For instance, a company from the Chinese province of Hei Long Jiang entered into a joint venture with a Vancouver trading company to sell skates, hockey sticks, furs and other products that are already made or manufactured in Canada. But the quality of their hockey equipment just cannot measure up to the high standards set by sports-supply firms marketing European- and North American–made hockey products in Canada. These firms, after all, have been marketing such products for years. Why the communist Chinese would now suddenly want to enter the highly competitive field is anyone's guess. Says Wang: "Some companies do not have the contracts and do not do the marketing feasibility studies." Even worse, the cash-strapped Chinese firms often have little choice but to deploy Chinese students studying business management in Canadian universities to develop their marketing strategies. The results are predictably inconsistent: some strategies work; others fail miserably.

Even copying success can lead to trouble. For example, the Chinese have tried to copy successful joint ventures, like the

Master Technology Corp. project, which assembles TVs from Chinese components in Canada. Many Asian executives mistakenly assume that they can sell TVs cheaper and sell a lot of them. But they have failed to realize that Canadian consumers will spend far more money for a brand name they can trust, rather than opt for an unknown, albeit cheaper product. They have also discounted the fact that North Americans want a guarantee that their televisions can be serviced after the sale. Such obstacles can be overcome. One Chinese firm sold $140 million worth of Chinese TV sets last year, 90 per cent of them in the United States.

Many of the Chinese trading companies peddling products in Canada are trying to market primitive and unattractive commodities. Says Wang: "The packing is terrible, usually a paper box or plain plastic wrapping. One company wanted to sell furniture that was made from sanded logs. The local Chinese would even say this is terrible."

More than just the recent boom in Hong Kong immigration is bringing in the communist Chinese. According to Xu Feng, the commercial consul at the Consulate of the People's Republic of China in Vancouver, many Chinese delegations have been lured to Vancouver, not by the high number of Hong Kong Chinese people living in the city, but because the city enhanced its reputation as a key part of the Pacific Rim during Expo 86. Says Feng: "Before 1986, only fifty delegations a year would visit Vancouver. Today, 500 delegations come every year." More people and delegations, says Feng, will likely come because they think that Canada has a good environment for doing business. China National Minerals and Mining Import and Export Corp., which set up an office in Vancouver in April, 1989, is an important example. Subsidiaries of China National Minerals and Mining are already doing business in Regina, where Sinotek Chemicals Ltd. and Sinotek International 1986 Inc. are located.

The effort to duplicate the success that Japan and other Asian power houses have enjoyed in Canada since the end of the Second World War will be a long, difficult and sometimes troubled one. In some cases, even the best intentions lead to impossible situations. One Chinese firm is attempting to crack the highly competitive North American furniture market by entering into a joint venture with a one-man cabinet-making firm called Minara Kitchens, originally owned by Tony Cerminara and his wife, in Concord, Ontario. Incredibly, to repeat the success of Asia's so-called Four Tigers, China has set about trying to learn how some businesses operate from the ground up. To that end, China sent four workers to Concord to learn their trade from Cerminara, making kitchen cabinets, bathroom vanities and laundry room cabinets. Cerminara cannot even communicate in Chinese with his workers, but he says: "I show them how with my hands." Unfortunately, business is slow at the moment and there is little for the trainees to do. "They are good people, they like to learn the way we do." All the good intentions at Cerminara's work bench will never help these four men take on the giants of the furniture trade.

Xu Feng says that there are several reasons for China's interest in Canada, and Canadian business would be wise to take note. Says Feng: "One purpose of being in Canada is because so many Western people could not understand the methods of business in China, so our offices here are trying to bridge the contacts to get a better understanding." To underline his point, Xu Feng loves to describe how an official with a large electronics firm in British Columbia made twelve trips to China to find a particular kind of ceramic insulator for hydroelectric equipment. He finally found it at home in Vancouver, at a trade show sponsored by a Chinese province. Feng's point, that he goes to such lengths to make, is that China's business ventures in Canada are helping Canadian business by bringing products to their doorstep — they no longer have to travel across vast stretches of China to find it. Feng laughs. "He spent a lot of money, then he found it at China trade fair in Vancouver."

Canadian businessmen working in various fields, particularly real estate development, would be wise to get to know some of these dynamic new Chinese business people, among them Shu

Mei Weng. Mei Weng, a civil engineer by training, is sixty-two, but looks no more than forty-five. The general manager of Toronto-based Great Wall International Investment (Canada) Ltd., she has launched more than $225 million worth of real estate development projects in Canada since she arrived in Toronto in June, 1987. By comparison, that is more than even most major Hong Kong developers have undertaken in Canada over the last five years. She works independently, but is open to working with Canadians because she loves to joint-venture on financing, in the same way that Cheng Yu-tung cuts Lee Shau-kee and Li Ka-shing in on many of his property deals. In this case, her financial partners are two larger developers from communist China, Sichuan-Huaxi Development Corp. and CITIC (China International Trust & Investment Corp.). This raises an important question: Where were the Canadian banks when Shu Mei Weng went looking for financing?

Her projects, after all, are as spectacular as any launched by The Three Musketeers. Her flagship project is a glittering $200-million Scarborough complex that includes two office towers, a five-star hotel, a condominium tower and a trade centre. She bought the land and devised the project independently, before bringing in Canadian developer CamRost. Like the Musketeers, she uses top local talent in her projects. Mei Weng's architect is the Kirkland Partnership, and she has hired top development lawyer Jane Pepino, both of Toronto. Says architect Ellis Galea-Kirkland: "Mei Weng is phenomenally sophisticated. She is very patient when she goes after something. When everyone else has given up."

Naturally, Mei Weng brings traditional *feng-shui* masters into the design process. That usually results in vast areas of landscaping between the buildings, as Galea-Kirkland puts it, "not to displease the land or the sky."

Another project being built by Mei Weng is a townhouse development in Richmond, B.C. It has been under construction since February, 1989, and is already sold out. She is also building a 300-unit, three-tower condominium development in Burnaby, B.C. Sounding very much like a typical Canadian developer, Mei Weng says: "I chose the Burnaby project because, in that area, there are lots of rental buildings and I think people there would like to try low-cost ownership." One can only wonder why Canadian developers are not beating a path to her doorstep; after all, if there was ever a time for "low-cost ownership," it is now.

Despite her age, Mei Weng plans to be involved in the Canadian property scene for years to come. She has bought land in Markham, Ontario, and will develop it at some future date. With, or without Canadian participation. And Mei Weng will not be alone in her drive to expand Chinese companies farther into the Canadian development game. She claims that other Chinese companies are now searching for prime real estate developments in Ontario. It can only be hoped that Canadian development firms will join her in her search. For his part, Stephen Yeung a director of Sichuan-Huaxi and CITIC has scouted a major residential housing property just to the north of Toronto in the booming city of Barrie.

As the communist Chinese become more involved in the Canadian economy, they quickly learn that this country's bureaucracy can be just as complicated as Beijing's. Mei Weng complains that her Scarborough project is still winding through the rezoning process, and her corporate masters in Beijing are growing more and more impatient by the day. Says Mei Weng: "My directors are quite frustrated back in China about the project. They cannot understand why it takes so long. They told me that, from now on when I do projects, they do not want any more deals that involve rezoning." Here again is a prime opening for a Canadian firm that has taken projects through the municipal planning bureaucracy — why not get involved with Mei Weng?

To say that Mei Weng can afford to be patient is a gross understatement: she is backed by one of the largest companies in China. And if that does not bring Canadian companies to her door to participate in a joint venture, what will? Great Wall is one of 180 subsidiaries working under the umbrella of the Shenzhen Special Economic Zone Development company, that has overseas operations in Hong Kong, the U.S. and Canada. It has built scores of commercial and residential projects, including hundreds of buildings in the Shenzhen Special Economic Zone. So it is not surprising that Mei Weng often thinks big — when she is drafting a new project. Indeed, 100-acre projects in Canada with multiple towers are the norm for this Chinese representative in Canada.

Of course, this Chinese expansion into Canada must be placed into the context of communist politics. To that end, former top communist business official, Sun Kaifeng, somewhat confusingly, anchors the company's expansion into North America to Marx and Engels's theory of historical determinism. Said Sun, in the firm's 1986 "Album" or annual report: "The timely decision-making of the policy to develop overseas business by our company just conforms to the great trend of world economic development and that must be a bright prospect." Canadian business would be wise to adapt to this latest twist in Marxist theory.

If developments undertaken by the Chinese in Los Angeles are the model for future, Canadians will be hearing more from Chinese business people like Mei Weng. She was able to use the Shenzhen economic zone's far-reaching assets when she completed a shopping centre development in Los Angeles for Great Wall. While other North American developers would have been scrambling for tenants, she simply requested that several other retail companies in the Shenzhen family open outlets in the mall, giving her instant leasing revenues, while at the same time keeping those revenues in the Shenzhen family. And that amounts to a corporate circle that few, if any, North American firm could muster.

The eventual scope of communist-Chinese investment in Canada is, however, difficult to assess, and any prediction must take into account the tenuous nature of Chinese economic reforms, particularly following the events of last May. Although China has privatized 85 per cent of its farming sector, it has not fully unleashed its manufacturing and fabricating business. Instead, it has only decentralized decision making and product supply, so that independent factories can be made more market-responsive. But once the industrial sector is cut free, some analysts say that Chinese investment in Canada will roar ahead. And that may lead to more advantages than appear on the surface. For instance, Galea-Kirkland points out an interesting difference between Hong Kong and Chinese business interests in Canada. Says Galea-Kirkland: "Unlike Hong Kong investment, Chinese investment does not bring an influx of immigration. So we are benefiting from the Chinese investment without having to deal with the problems of immigration."

Galea-Kirkland just may be right. The Bank of China is preparing an application for Schedule B bank status which, if successful, would allow it to participate fully in Canada's commercial bank sector. In the meantime, it is promoting trade and economic cooperation between Canada and China. "We are here," said Chao-Hua Du, chief representative for the Bank of China in Canada, "because more and more Chinese companies are coming to Canada. People will come to make remittances to families back home and we will be used in the increasing trade between China and Canada."

The communist Chinese are also here to learn. This is another area where Canadian business can not only help, but also earn a profit. Unlike Mai Weng and Great Wall, which independently planned and set up its Scarborough development, China State Construction Engineering Corp. has come into Canada as a mere supporting player and student in the development of the palatial Chestnut Park Hotel in downtown

Toronto. In the fifty-fifty deal for the $100-million hotel in Toronto's downtown Chinatown, China State Construction has invested simply in order to learn how to build sophisticated Western-style hotels at home in China. Fred Braida, the leading partner in the deal, said that the company has contributed $20 million, is helping to carry the financing and is designing a Chinese garden for the terrace roof.

China State Construction is also sending ten groups of employees for six-month stints in the hotel to learn about such things as housekeeping, front desk service, kitchen equipment and art selection. A group of six chefs also visited. Consider this: those six state employees are just a few of the 1.5 million people on China's state payroll. In China and the Third World, particularly Africa, the company has built everything from stadiums to hospitals, factories to housing.

Fred Braida, a Toronto hotelier who owns and operates Carlton Place Hotel near Toronto's Pearson International Airport and who operates the Carlton Inn Hotel in downtown Toronto, says the company approached him after seeing his consulting work on the Toronto Beijing Hotel in Beijing. "Like everything else with China there is a need to learn through contributing. Their hotels in China are more like YMCAs. Now they want to copy us. I was honored to be chosen. This company has the key to development in Asia. They have the ability to supply everything from engineering on up. But they are in Canada to learn — they do not want to take over."

When China State Construction chairman Tao Jin Tang cut the ribbon for the hotel's gala opening in April, 1989, the trainees stood out from the rest of Braida's employees. Dressed in oversized mismatched suits, with the sleeves grazing the knuckles of their hands, they appeared shy and rustic. Guo Baolin is one of the current trainees. A graduate of the Institute of Foreign Languages in Beijing, he speaks relatively good English and has taken a particular interest in the computer reservation system. "In comparison, our hotels are not as modern. We come here to learn the business. We were sent out to broaden our minds; to see what we have not." Baolin was amazed by Braida's participation with the trainees. "He works all the time physically. This you cannot find in China," he says. But Baolin also says that even after a year of exposure, China State is still not ready to build its own Western-style hotel in China.

China State has other North American projects, including a shopping complex in Montreal's Chinatown. Now Braida and the company are working together in a joint venture to build a hotel at Kennedy Airport. As well, the Chinese have been sinking a large amount of their investment money into natural resource projects in an effort to secure long-term supplies of pulp, petrochemicals and coal. The largest example to date: the $94-million purchase of a pulp mill in Castlegar, B.C., in 1987 by CITIC B.C. Inc. a subsidiary of Beijing-based China International Trust & Investment Corp., along with Montreal-based Power Corp. of Canada and Consolidated-Bathurst Inc. CITIC is a massive conglomerate with more than a hundred subsidiaries.

CITIC officials say that another large Canadian project in the resource sector is under negotiation, and will likely be announced in the fall of 1989. At the same time, CITIC president Teisheng Cui said that his company has considered an investment in the Potash Corp. of Saskatchewan, when the Saskatchewan government privatizes the company, but the most likely bidder is the large Chinese conglomerate China Agribusiness Investment Co., which is interested in obtaining a more secure supply of potash, used as fertilizer, for China.

Clearly, two great economic forces are gearing up to wash over Canada as the century draws to a close. On the one hand, there is a revolution under way in Canada. Two of the nation's great city's — Vancouver and Toronto — will be changed forever.

For its part, Vancouver is being slowly transformed from a sleepy provincial city, where people either retired after a long life of work, or young people retired to escape a long life of work, and where logging, unions and the province's celebrated politics commanded the headlines, into a vibrant bustling city dominated by its new Asian citizens. Vancouver has longed to be known as Canada's gateway to the Pacific Rim. Well, the Pacific Rim is sending its best citizens and Vancouver, despite some brutish outbursts, is adapting well.

In Toronto, the impact is not as dramatic, but that is only because the Hong Kong Chinese have been swallowed up in the city's polyglot mix. But a walk down the narrow streets of the city's commercial quarter is like a walking into almost any bank in Hong Kong's frantic business district: the smiling curious eyes that rise to greet you are almost always Asian. And beneath the dim wraith of pollution hanging over the city's endless plain of dreary suburbs, Canada's richest immigrants are erecting giant "superhomes" and filling them with family and the treasures of their past lives in Hong Kong.

The challenge for Canadians is twofold: do we accept these new immigrants who seem somehow threatening as they speed by in their BMWs while conducting business over their car telephones, as we did waves of British and Western European immigrants in the past. Or do we ignore the great and most exciting events of our time — that technology has reduced the world to village size — and our greatest enjoyment, both spiritual and intellectual, should flow from welcoming all our neighbors, whatever their color. To accept the great flood of British, and later American money that has historically flowed into Canada, but to reject the new tide of Hong Kong money, would mean that we have stopped growing as a nation. We would be little more than thick-necked hillbillies, lacking both vision and reason.

But Hong Kong money also poses a second challenge to Canadian businessmen, this one from the likes of the powerful Three Musketeers and from other less wealthy Hong Kong residents. Nova Corporation's Robert Blair accepted the challenge years ago, when he wandered the streets of Hong Kong, firm in the knowledge that, there in the narrow streets of the financial district, were new, and spectacular, opportunities for corporate Canada. One need not always look to pigeon-chested Bay Street for financing.

But Blair's successful foray into Hong Kong was just a beginning. As the countdown to 1997 begins in earnest, more and more of the colony's top business people will be looking to Canada for economic shelter and new business opportunities. And each time one of these new millionaire refugees arrives, he brings new and lucrative options for Canada's business sector today — and for Canada tomorrow. As one top immigration official put it, Canada is really importing a whole new strata of super entrepreneurs who will inject new vitality into the country.

INDEX

aerospace industry, 175
AGIFEL Properties, 143
Air China, 196
Aird, John Black, 115
Albernia Place, 144
Alberta, 20, 47, 81, 83, 94, 95, 104
Alcan Asia Ltd., 184
Allied Holdings Ltd., 144
American Telephone & Telegraph
  Co., 122
Annley Fashions, 101-02
Anti-Chinese Association, 89
Asia Pacific Business Institute, 123
Asia-Pacific Initiative, 158, 187-88
Asiatic Exclusion League, 155-56
astronauts, 172
Atkins, Marty, 83
Au Bak Ling, 144
Australia, 19, 21, 81, 106

Bank of British Columbia, 20
Bank of China, 80, 196, 203
Bank of Nova Scotia, 184

B.C. Chamber of Commerce, 158
Berton, Pierre, 88
Blair, Robert, 33, 44-45, 46, 175-76,
  206-07
Bourassa, Robert, 96, 105, 106
Braida, Fred, 204-05
British Columbia: Asia-Pacific
  Initiative, 158, 187-88; business
  immigrants, 100, 103; communist-
  Chinese investments in, 195, 196;
  development of Expo lands, 47-52;
  economic priorities, 97-98; effect of
  Asian investment on economy,
  146-47; efforts to attract wealthy
  business immigrants, 19, 20, 81, 83,
  94, 104, 158-59; forestry, 24; history
  of Chinese in, 86-89; oil and gas
  industry, 76; racism toward Chinese
  citizens, 108, 154; students lured to,
  20
British-European Immigration Aid
  Foundation, 108, 153
Broadfoot, Bob, 5-6

Brown, Bob, 84
business immigrants: attracted by
experts in professional firms, 188-89;
bureaucratic load, 191; challenge
offered by, 206-07; countries
competing for, 106-07; federal and
provincial governments attract
wealthy, 2, 19-20, 81-83; in Toronto,
118-22; in Vancouver, 143-45;
initiatives to attract, 187-88;
interested in property and
manufacturing, 191; investor
category, 94-99; joint ventures with,
186-87; lack of information after
admission, 100-03; negotiation
techniques, 135; public backlash
against, 107-08; qualifications for
investors, 94-99; statistics on, 83-84;
straddling East and West, 172-74;
tax avoidance, 190-91, 192; types of
enterprises, 84-85, 122-23, 147
Business Immigration Program, 81-82,
85, 92-93, 119; flaws, 99-103; tool for
regional development, 103-04
Business Migrant Program, 106
Burrard International Holdings, 161

Campbell, Gordon, 150
CamRost, 200
Canada: appeal of, for Hong Kong
Chinese, 20-21, 83; enterprises with
China, 26, 174-78, 194-205; family
connections used for flow of money
into, 45-46; history of Chinese in,
86-91; history of Li's relationship to,
38-40; impact of influx, 24-26; Li's
investments in, 32-36, 44-52;
students from Hong Kong, 20, 25
Canada Packers Inc., 184
Canada Systems Group Ltd., 66
Canada-U.S. Free Trade Agreement,
25
Canadian Broadcasting Corp., 150

Canadian business: Bank of China,
196; bureaucratic load, 191;
challenge offered by immigrants,
206-07; China's interest in, 199;
enterprises with China, 194-205;
initiatives to court Asian investors,
187-88; joint ventures, 186-87;
political subtleties involved, 190;
professional firms hire experts,
188-90; tax avoidance on Hong
Kong assets, 190-91, 192
Canadian Imperial Bank of
Commerce, 32, 41, 46, 98, 184-85,
196
Canadian International Properties
Ltd., 167
Canadian Maple Leaf Fund Ltd., 98
Canadian Pacific Railway, 87-88, 143
Canadian Wheat Board, 197
Canterra Energy, 33
Cathay Pacific Airways, 18
Celanese Far East Ltd., 184
Central Garments, 120
Cerminara, Tony, 199
Chak-lim Raymond Cheng, 120
Chan, Caleb, 146, 160-62
Chan, Howard, 119
Chan, M.Y., 188
Chan, Patrick, 118
Chan, Peggy, 67, 119
Chan, Tom, 161
Chao-Hua Du, 203
Charity Through Fashion, 114
Chau Frank, 128-30, 173-74
Chen, Julia, 173
Chen, Norman, 127
Cheng, Henry and Peter, 73
Cheng, James, 159, 186
Cheng, Joseph, 22
Cheng Yu-tung, 3, 25, 33, 43-44, 49,
54-57, 61, 67, 70-78, 115, 124, 130,
131, 135, 142, 186
Cheung, Johnny, 147

Cheung Kong (Holdings) Ltd., 37, 39-40, 43, 62
Chestnut Park Hotel, 203-04
China. *See* People's Republic of China
China Agribusiness Investment Co., 205
China Civil Engineering Corp., 38
China Everbright Holdings Co. Ltd., 18
China International Trust and Investment Corp. (CITIC), 18, 38, 200, 205
China National Minerals and Mining Import and Export Corp., 198
China Resources, 37
China State Construction Engineering Corp., 203-05
Chinatown Centre, 118
Chinatown International Chinese Restaurant, 118
Chinese Businessmen's Executive Network, 114
Chinese Canadians: illegal immigrants, 90-91; Second World War, 90, 157; Toronto community, 111-17; Vancouver community, 143-45, 156-57; view of Ottawa's program, 85-86
Chinese Exclusion Act, 156
Chinese Immigration Act, 89-90, 116
Chinese in Canada, The, 154
Ching Chun Bao, 122
Chow, Olivia, 113
Chow Tai Fook Enterprises, 72
Chu, Danny, 102
Chu, David, 122
Chung, Thomas, 61-62
Churchill, Sir Winston, 38
CITIC. *See* China International Trust and Investment Corp.
Colapinto, Marion, 113
Colliers Macaulay Nicholls Inc., 146, 193

Collins, Douglas, 150
Commission for Canada in Hong Kong, 19, 21, 81
Concord Pacific Developments, 48, 142
condominiums, 123-24, 134, 145, 149, 161
Consolidated-Bathurst Inc., 205
Connell, George, 25
Constellation Hotel, 125-26
Consumers Distributing Co. Ltd., 64, 65, 66
Copthorne Holdings Inc., 124
Couvelier, Mel, 158
Crown Life Insurance Co., 185
Cullen-Coulture Agreement, 105

DataCrown Corp., 66
Deng Xiaoping, 17
Doder, Louise, 181
Doo, William, 55, 71, 72, 74, 77, 136
Dragon City Mall, 115, 118, 128

Emigrant, The, 81
Eng, Andrea, 146, 150, 188, 192-94
Eng, Peter, 144

Fairchild Developments Ltd., 144
Fairclough, Ellen, 91
Fang Zheng Ping, 18
fashion industry, 25, 67, 101-02, 119, 120-21
federal government: Asia-Pacific Initiative, 158, 187; business immigrants, 92-98; Business Immigration Program, 82-83, 92-98, 119; Chinese Immigration Act, 89-90, 116; Chinese immigration policy, 86-91; efforts to attract wealthy immigrants, 81-86; flaws in immigration program, 99-103; head tax, 88-89; passport policy, 2-3, 23-24, 96

feng-shui, 131-34, 200
Ferguson, Louis, 85, 96, 99, 102-03
Financial Times, 176
First Generation Resources Ltd., 98, 99
Fisher, Alex, 112
Fook-Shui Li, Ronald, 115
Fortune, 35
Fraser Institute, 147, 186
From China to Canada, 88
Fung, Thomas, 144
Funk, Steven, 98, 99

Galea-Kirkland, Ellis, 200, 203
Gaw, Danny, 144
Georgia Hotel, 146, 161
Georgian Towers, 164
gold rush, 86
Goldberg, Michael, 143, 147, 188
Golden Harvest Studios, 122
Goldsmith, Sir James, 43
Goldyear Realty Inc., 129
Gorges, Howard, 182
Grande Residence, La, 67
Gray Beverage, 162, 163
Great Wall International Investment (Canada) Ltd., 174, 200, 202
Green Island Cement Co. Ltd., 40
Green, Mendel, 134, 136
Guandong province, 23, 185-86
Guay, Jean-Pierre, 50
Guo Baoli, 204-05

Harbour Castle Westin, 124
head tax, 88-89
Heaven's Gates, 100
Heap, Dan, 99
Henderson Land, 41
Heng Seng Index, 5, 182
Hildebrand, Barton, 104
Hill, Norman & Associates Ltd., 134-35
Ho, David, 162

Ho, Flora, 58, 59
Ho Fook, 57
Ho Kwong, 58
Ho Leung, 58
Ho, Lucina, 67, 68-70, 119-20, 173
Ho, Pansy, 67-70
Ho, Rita, 163
Ho Sai-Wing, 58
Ho Saiu-yiu, 58
Ho, Stanley, 3, 16, 33, 54, 56-61, 67-70, 71, 77, 114, 122, 130, 184; gambling empire in Macau, 61-63; Semi-Tech, 63-66
Hotung, Sir Robert, 58
Hong Kong: administration of, 14; agreement for return to China, 15-16; bad etiquette for professionals to desert, 190; businessmen's view of Canada, 82; Canadian citizens in, 13-14, 82, 173; Canadian companies operating in, 184-85; China's offshore investment, 195; connection in trade between Canada and China, 177-78, 196-97; concern about future under China, 21-23, 77-78, 180-83; continued investment in, 56; description of, 10-13; exodus to Canada, 2-3, 20-21; flood of money to Canada, 18-19, 98; government opposes Canadian immigration program, 85; history of, 22; importance of feng-shui, 131-34; marriage law, 69 ; role in unified China, 184; Second World War, 38-39; students in Canada, 20, 25
Hong Kong and China Gas Co., 76
Hong Kong and Shanghai Banking Corp., 17, 20, 35, 42, 43, 132
HongKong Bank, 38
HongKong Bank of Canada, 4, 84, 142
Hong Kong Canadian Club, 34
Hong Kong Convention and Exhibition Centre, 71

Hong Kong Electric Holdings Ltd., 40
Hong Kong Land, 38
Hong Kong Securities Commission, 95
Hong Kong Stock Exchange, 15, 17, 36, 62, 65, 75, 123, 181-82
hotels, 67, 124-26, 145-46
Hou, Edward, 105
housing market: in Vancouver, 148-50, 168-69, 188
Hsin Kuang restaurants, 118-19, 133
Huckride, Frits, 147
Hughes, Jack, 101
Hui, Ernest, 164, 191-92
Hung, Daniel, 118, 127-28
Hung, Edward, 95
Hung, Henry, 118, 127-28
Hung, Patrick, 122
Husky Oil, 32, 33, 43, 45-47, 48, 160
Hutchinson Whampoa Ltd., 36, 38, 40, 42, 43

immigrants: benefits seen from Asian, 186-87; history of Chinese, 86-91, 115-17; illegal, 90-91. *See also* business immigrants
Immigration Act, 102-03
immigration policy: Business Immigration Program, 81-82, 85, 92-98, 119; changed in 1960s, 91-92, 157-58; flaws in program, 99-103; from 1923-59, 89-91; head tax, 88-89; passport policy, 2-3, 23-24, 96; public backlash against, 107-08
Imperial Fashions Co. Ltd., 120-21
Inco Pacific Ltd., 184
International Financial Centre, 188
International Semi-Tech Microelectronics Inc., 26, 49, 57, 63-66, 68, 122

Jack Canuck, 116
Jansen, John, 159, 188

Japanese Canadians, 90
Jardine Matheson, 8, 17, 43, 58
Johnson, Graham, 88, 154
joint ventures: with China, 194, 197-99; with Hong Kong immigrants, 186-88, 192-93
Jung, Douglas, 157

Kalmar, George, 126
Kaufman, Harvey, 134-35
Kennedy, Jack, 35
Keswick, Simon, 37
KHK Fashion Group Inc., 67, 119
Kim Lan Loretta Yip, 122
King Fok Jewelers, 127
King, Mackenzie, 90
Koh, John, 182
Ku Klux Klan, 156
Kuok, Eliza, 67, 119-20
Kuok, Robert, 146
Kwan, Eugene, 188, 189
Kwok, Ezra, 30, 31, 34, 48
Kwok, Norma, 44-45
Kwong, Francis, 129

Lam, David, 153, 166-69
Lam Foundation, 167-68
Lansdowne Park Shopping Centre, 143
Lap Lee, 122
Lau, Geoffrey, 160
Laurier Institute, 187
Layton, Jack, 113
Lee, David, 142
Lee, John, 189-91
Lee Shau-kee, 3, 41, 49, 55-56, 61, 72, 73, 75-77, 130, 131, 142, 186
Leong, Lincoln and Winston, 143
Leong, Sydney, 143
Li Ka-shing, 3, 15 16, 24, 26, 31-32, 43-44, 55, 61, 71, 73, 75, 76, 124, 130, 142-43, 175; Canadian investments, 32-36; development of Expo lands in

Vancouver, 33, 47-52; history of relationship with Canada, 38-40; Husky deal, 44-47, 48; Hutchinson buyout, 42-43; relationship with Beijing, 36-38
Li Peng, 180, 182, 183
Li, Peter, 89, 154
Li, Robert, 37, 45-46, 175
Li, Ronald, 183
Li, Victor, 31, 33, 37, 45-47, 48, 50-52, 149, 160, 175
Liu, Kwai Cheong (Casey), 162-64
Lo Ka-shui, 125
Lo, Vincent, 125, 126
Lo Ying-shek, 125
Lo Yuk Sui, 125-26
LuCliff Place, 126
Lussier, Gaétan, 100

MacArthur, Robert, 145
Macau, 60, 63
Macdonald, Sir John A., 87
Maclean's, 34, 116, 181, 183
MacMillan Bloedel (Asia) Ltd., 184
Magee Secondary School, 151
Magnetic Electronics Inc., 122
Magnus, George, 44, 47, 49, 51
Mainland Gas Service, 76
Malarek, Victor, 100
Mandarin Club, 114-15
Manitoba, 81, 94, 103
Manufacturers Life Insurance Co. of Canada, 185
Master Technology Corp., 198
Mavalwala, Jamshed, 91
Max's Donuts Ltd., 144
McLean, Walter, 94, 96, 101
Merbanco Group, 99
Meridien Hotel, Le, 67, 126
Minara Kitchens, 199
Minichiello, Peter, 151
Mississauga Chinese Centre, 129
Mitsubishi Corp., 122

Montreal, 81, 100, 105
Mulroney, Brian, 93, 94, 96, 114
Murray, Simon, 44, 47

Napier, Lord, 22
Nash, Alan, 103, 106-07
Nathwani, Rashmi, 135
Nendick, David, 5
New Brunswick, 2, 94, 103
New China News Agency, 182
Newfoundland, 94, 103
New World Developments, 71, 72, 74
New World Harbourside Hotel, 74
Ng, Wilson, 98
Noble House, 114
Northern Telecom (Asia) Ltd., 184
Northwest Territories, 103
Nova Corp., 33, 44

Onderdonk, Andrew, 87
Ontario: business immigrants, 103; economic priorities, 98; efforts to attract wealthy business immigrants, 81, 83, 94, 95, 104; history of Chinese immigration, 115-17
Ontario Ministry of Industry, Trade and Technology, 101, 104
Opium War, 22
Oriental Ocean restaurant, 133

Pacific Palisades Hotel, 146
Pacific Place, 33, 48
Pacific Rim Gas, 75
Paliburg Investments, 125
Palmer, Arnold, 55
passport policy, 2-3, 23-24, 96
People's Republic of China: active participant in Canadian economy, 26; agreement for return of Hong Kong to, 15-16; concern about future under, 21-23; economy of, 178-79; exporting activity in Guangdong province, 23, 185;

future of Ho's gambling empire, 61-63; Hutchinson buyout, 42-43; interest in enterprises with Canada, 174-78, 194-205; Li's investment in, 36-38; rebellion in Tiananmen Square, 2, 4, 180-83; Semi-Tech agreement, 64-66; strategy of billionaires for continued prosperity, 56-57, 77-78; vast pool of cheap labor, 184; views Hong Kong as foreign-currency generator, 17-18

Pepino, Jane, 200
Phillips, William, 182
Polysar Ltd., 33
Potash Corp. of Saskatchewan, 205
Power Corp. of Canada, 205
Prince Edward Island, 94, 98, 103
Princess Alexandra, 36
provincial governments: cash for citizenship, 94; determine qualifications for funds and projects, 104; efforts to attract wealthy immigrants, 2, 18-20, 81-83; interprovincial competition, 104-05

Quebec: efforts to attract wealthy immigrants, 2, 19, 20, 81, 83, 94, 95, 103, 104-06; language law, 50, 105-06

racial discrimination: history of, against Chinese, 86-91; in Australia, 106-07; in Ontario, 74, 115-16; in Vancouver, 24, 51-52, 139, 141, 150-57, 168-69
Ramada Hotel-Airport West, 126
real estate: broaden choice of investments, 188; communist China's interest in, 194-95, 199-202; feng-shui, 131-34; in Toronto, 123-37; in Vancouver, 144-51, 194-95
Real Estate Institute of Canada, 123
recession of 1981-82, 19-20

Regal hotel chain, 125-26
regional development, 103-04
Reichmanns, 73
Robbie, D.W., 184-85
Royal Bank of Canada, 184
Royal Canadian Mounted Police, 91
Royal Commission on Chinese Immigration, 87, 88
Royal LePage, 148

St. Germain Bakery, 144
Saltwater City, 155
Sandberg, Michael, 42, 115
San Francisco Ramada Renaissance, 162
Saskatchewan, 94, 103
Saturday Night, 116
Scheller, Zenon, 145
Schultz, Robert, 191
Seagram (China) Ltd., 184
Second World War, 38-39, 90, 157
Shakespeare, Noah, 89
Shaw, Lucy, 164-65
Shaw, Sir Run Run, 165
Shenzhen Electronics Group, 65
Shenzhen Special Economic Zone Development Co., 174, 202
Shiu Pong Enterprises, 128
Shu Mai Weng, 200-02
Shui On Group, 126
Sian, Sally Au, 144
Sian Tao Group, 144
Sichuan-Huaxi Development Corp., 200
Sin Tak-fun, 58
Sing Tao, 123
Singer Sewing Machine Co; 64, 66, 122
Singapore Hyatt Regency, 132
Sinotek Chemicals Ltd., 198
Sinotek International 1986 Inc., 198
Sizzling Pan Chinese Restaurant, 120

Smith, Janet, 156
Sociedade de Turismo e Diversoes de
  Macau, 61
South China Morning Post, 14, 50, 106
South Korea, 178, 185
Soviet Union, 179
Stikeman Elliott, 188, 189
stock market crash of October, 1987,
  14-15, 75, 182
students: in Vancouver school,
  151-52; university, from Hong Kong,
  20, 25
Sun Hung Kai Securities, 144
Sun Kaifeng, 202
Sun Life Assurance Co. of Canada,
  185
Sung, Alfred, 120
Sung, Siu-kwong, 80
Supreme Court of Canada: French-
  only sign law, 106
Swire Pacific, 43

Taiping Rebellion, 86
Taiwan, 178, 185
Tak Chen, 129
Tang Wai Yin and Sun Yin, 120-21
Tao Jin Tang, 204
Tattler, 14
Texaco Canada, 33
Teisheng Cui, 205
Thatcher, Margaret, 36
Thorne Ernst & Whinney, 189-90
Tiananmen Square, 2, 4, 180-83
Tin Shui Wai development, 37
Ting, James, 26, 64-66, 121-22, 184
Tsang, Dorothy and Peter, 173
Tse, Patrick and Deborah, 144, 159
Toronto, 20, 21, 100, 105; business
  immigrants, 118-22; changing city,
  206; Chinese Canadian community
  in, 111-17; real estate market in,
  123-37, 194-95
Toronto Harbour Commission, 130

UBC Golf Club, 162-63
Union Faith, 46
United Kingdom: founding of Hong
  Kong, 14, 17
United States, 19, 21, 81, 107, 195
University of Toronto, 14, 25, 72

Vancouver, 20, 21, 24, 32, 45, 105;
  accessibility of Chinese community
  to Canadian businessmen, 187;
  changed by Hong Kong money,
  141-42, 186, 205-06; Chinese
  community in, 143-45; communist-
  Chinese companies in, 196, 198;
  development of Expo lands, 33,
  47-54, 142-43; Ho's hotels in, 67;
  influx of immigrants in post-war
  period, 157; International Financial
  Centre, 188; racial discrimination,
  24, 51-52, 139, 141, 150-57, 168-69;
  reaction to influx of Asian wealth,
  148; real estate in, 144-51, 194-95;
  tension between new and old
  immigrants, 165-66
Vancouver Province, 51, 142
Vancouver Sun, 108, 142
Vander Zalm, William, 50-51, 75, 142,
  159
Vassos, Don, 149
Vincci Watch International Corp.,
  147
Volrich, Jack, 153
Vonnegut, Kurt, 186

Walker, Michael, 147, 186-87
Wang, Jackson, 196-98
Webster, Jack, 151
Wharton Renaissance Hotel, 126
Wilson, Michael, 114
Wilson, Sir David, 5, 75
Wisebrod, Avi, 123, 135-36
Wisener, Robert, 99

Women and Girls Protection Act, 156
Wong, Clifford, 126-27
Wong, K.K., 144
Wong, Mary-Jean, 127
Wong, Michael, 73-74, 131
Wong, Robert, 113
Woo, Edward, 144
Wyllie, William, 42, 125

Xu Feng, 198-99

Yee, Gary, 86
Yee, Paul, 155-156
Yeung, C.W., 127
Yeung, Stephen, 172, 174, 201
Yip, Ivan, 132-33
Yip, William, 94
Yue-long Pao, Sir, 16-17
Yukon, 103

Zhao Ziyang, 180, 183